IN THE LIGHT OF THE CROSS

IN THE LIGHT
OF THE CROSS

HAROLD COOKE PHILLIPS

ABINGDON-COKESBURY PRESS
New York • *Nashville*

IN THE LIGHT OF THE CROSS

In Loving Tribute

TO
MY FATHER

George Wallace Phillips
whom I do not remember
yet have never forgotten

PREFACE

THIS BOOK grew out of a series of Jarrell Foundation lectures given at the Candler School of Theology, Emory University, Atlanta, Georgia, during Ministers' Week, January 21 to 25, 1946. Since their delivery the lectures have been expanded and two chapters have been added in order to complete the theme—the one on the Sadducees and the one on the Public.

An impression that remains even more vivid in my mind than the Georgia pines silhouetted against the deep blue Atlanta sky is the friendliness of those with whom it was my good fortune to associate during that week at Emory University. Adequately to express my appreciation I should have to mention each member of the faculty, and I do so implicitly as I thank Dean and Mrs. H. B. Trimble for their many courtesies, and President and Mrs. Goodrich White for the gracious hospitality of their lovely home, in which I had the privilege of being entertained. I must not forget either those who attended the lectures; their sympathetic and understanding spirit turned what might have been a heavy chore into an inspiring experience.

My indebtedness to others in the preparation of the book is greater than the footnotes would indicate. I must especially thank President George P. Michaelides of Schauffler College, Cleveland, for reading the chapters and making some valuable suggestions; also Mrs. M. D. Phillips and my tireless secretary, Miss Gladys Dray, for their painstaking work on the manuscript.

HAROLD C. PHILLIPS

CONTENTS

The Cross of Christ must be, either the darkest spot of all in the mystery of existence, or a searchlight by the aid of which we may penetrate the surrounding gloom.
—BURNETT H. STREETER

What Crucified Jesus?

THE QUESTION "Who crucified Jesus?" is a moot and, in my opinion, a wholly irrelevant one. Gentiles have blamed the Jews, and Jews the Romans; so Adam blamed Eve and Eve the serpent. This approach is unilluminating. It misses the point. It starts on the wrong foot—certainly on the wrong assumption. For it singles out a particular race or people and tends to regard them as more grossly cruel or stupid than some other group similarly placed would have been. Such an assumption is false and has little if any evidence to support it. The Cross sheds no light at all on biology or race. It does, however, shed a flood of light on the sin of the human heart, and sin is a malady which involves all mankind. Perhaps the real question is not "Who crucified Jesus?" but *"What* crucified Jesus?" This book attempts to answer that question.

For fear, however, that the answer may seem evasive, let me say that to the best of my knowledge—my knowledge may be far from the best—the Pharisees and Sadducees, that is to say, the religiously conservative and socially and politically privileged of Jesus' day, were primarily responsible for his crucifixion. That this should cause Christians to malign the Jewish people or to regard them as arch sinners is stupid. Does anyone condemn the Greeks for the martyrdom of Socrates or Americans for the assassination of Lincoln? Such an attitude, however, is more than stupid. It is sheer hypocrisy. It assumes that had Jesus been born

11

a Gentile and lived among Gentiles he would have experienced a different fate. Such an assumption is utterly baseless. There is not a particle of truth in it.

While therefore I must of necessity refer in these pages to individuals and groups of the first-century world, both Jews and Romans, who were involved in the crucifixion, I am not thinking of them as Jews or Romans but as human beings like you and me, reacting in typical and characteristic human fashion. The negro spiritual asks "Were you there when they crucified my Lord?" The answer is "Yes," because it was human sin that crucified Jesus, and no one race or people has any monopoly on that.

It is clear that the evils which sent Jesus to his cross, and which from that day to this "crucify . . . the Son of God afresh," are not the evils the church habitually or readily recognizes as sins. The church has been quick to condemn the sins of the flesh. The Master, we may be sure, did not make light of these. No one who placed such singular value on human personality could regard as trivial those evils which destroy both the body and soul of man. The truth is, however, that it was not these evils which sent Christ to his cross. The evils that led to his crucifixion were for the most part the respectable ones—so respectable indeed that to be guilty of them was not to be considered a sinner in Jesus' day any more than in ours. Yet it is these sins which are "in good and regular standing" from which perchance the cause of Christ has most to fear. The wolf in sheep's clothing is the most dangerous wolf.

The nature of this study makes it necessary for us to approach the Cross from an *ethical* standpoint. The death of Jesus is more often discussed theologically than ethically.

12

This is as it should be. For it is only on the assumption that Jesus bore a unique relationship to God and has revealed most fully the nature and purpose of God that a discussion of the ethical forces in which he was involved has any particular significance. Many great and good men before him, and since, have died for the truth. Yet the fact is that the death of Jesus has exerted an influence on human history unequaled by that of any other great or good man. We are therefore compelled to believe that the difference between his death and that of other brave and noble souls is due to the great difference between Jesus and other men. It may be difficult to put this difference into words, but it is impossible to deny that it exists. Paul voiced it well when he said that "God was in Christ, reconciling the world unto himself." It is therefore only on the assumption that Jesus' life has implications for us which are vastly more revealing and meaningful than any other life that we are justified in considering the evils that opposed him, sought to destroy him, and over which he lives in deathless triumph.

No one, I suppose, will be more aware than I that the subjects here discussed deserve a much more thorough treatment than I have been able to give them. If, however, these chapters help to delineate those areas of our life which have yet to be brought within the redemptive purpose of God, and to shed some light on what such redemption involves, the book will have served its purpose.

I

Ecclesiasticism: *The Pharisees*

THE MOST revealing fact about the crucifixion of Jesus is that among the primary actors in that drama were good people, church people—the Pharisees. This fact becomes all the more significant when we realize that the Pharisees acted in good faith and were unquestionably conscientious. Jesus referred to them as "hypocrites." He did not, I am sure, mean to infer that they all were. Not all the Pharisees were hypocrites, any more than all church people are today. The Master himself realized that people, though conscientious in their motives, could commit grave wrongs, and he warned his disciples: "The time cometh, that whosoever killeth you will think that he doeth God service." [1] We must then confront the fact that sometimes the most determined and aggressive opposition to truth springs not from those who avowedly betray it but from those who professedly defend it. The foes of truth are often they of her own household. Judgment must begin at the house of God. Let us begin our study there.

A typical reaction of these church people to the message and ministry of Jesus is expressed in the words that his disciples once put to him: "Knowest thou that the Pharisees were offended?" It is perhaps not an exaggeration to say that the crucifixion of Jesus was due primarily to the fact

---

[1] I shall quote fairly often from John's Gospel. I realize that such quotations may represent an interpretation rather than the *ipsissima verba* of Jesus. They seem to me, however, to be in accord with the spirit of Jesus as it is revealed in the New Testament.

that he offended the Pharisees, the church people of his day. The Pharisees were religiously the most influential group of Palestinian Judaism. They were not, however, the only group.

There were the Zealots, the ultrapatriots of their day, the popular patriotic party. They hated the rich and powerful ruling classes. Particularly did they hate the Romans who ruled their country. The Zealots were people of great courage and devotion, with an admirable love of freedom. However, in their zeal to cast off the Roman yoke they came to identify religion with nationalism, and went at times to fanatical extremes. They were the hundred per cent patriots.

Another group was the Essenes. Though numerically small, they nonetheless exerted a great influence. They were a peace-loving people of high ethical standards. Interested in agriculture, they lived simply and frugally. They were given to asceticism and an otherworldly outlook. It is thought that John the Baptist belonged to this group.

The Sadducees comprised a third group. They were the aristocrats of early Judaism, and belonged to the priestly class that officiated in the temple. They were wealthy and worldly-minded, and so were not greatly concerned about religious matters. They did not believe in the survival of the soul, the resurrection of the dead, or the existence of angels or spirits. They had no belief in divine providence, as far at least as it was related to the individual, though they did not deny the possibility of a general overruling providence. Their primary interest lay in social and political matters.

And there were the Pharisees. Of all the groups the Pharisees were by far the most representative of Palestinian Judaism in the time of Christ. There were approximately a million Jews in Palestine during Jesus' earthly life. Of this number about six thousand were Pharisees, but they exerted an influence far beyond their numerical strength. The majority of the Jews, even if not identified with the Pharisaic party, were Pharisees in belief. Josephus wrote: "Whatsoever they [the people] do about divine worship or prayers or sacrifices, they perform according to their direction." "Have any of . . . the Pharisees believed on him?" asked the populace, indicating that they regarded the Pharisees as the key to the situation. John on two occasions almost identified the Jews as a whole with the Pharisees.[2] Nor would he have been far wrong, for in Jesus' day Judaism and Pharisaism were almost synonymous terms.[3]

While Jesus did not identify himself with any of these groups, it may fairly be said that he was nearest to the Pharisees, as he was probably farthest from the Sadducees; for the Pharisees, let us remember, were the religious leaders of their day. They were sincere, high-principled, conscientious folk. They believed in God, in prayer, in divine providence, in the resurrection. They worshiped. So missionary-minded were they that Jesus once said to them, "Ye compass sea and land to make one proselyte." Yet these good people, respectable people, church people, became Jesus' bitterest enemies. They sent spies to oppose him and at length to betray him to the Romans. They roused the Nazarenes to cast him out. They tried to catch him by tricky questions

[2] John 1:19; 2:18.
[3] For fuller treatment of these four groups see Joseph Klausner, *Jesus of Nazareth*, pp. 204 ff.

like those dealing with tribute money and with the Commandments, they supported the chief priests in the last assault upon Jesus, and finally they sealed the stone of his tomb lest the "deceiver" should escape. To the Pharisees the prophet of Nazareth was Public Enemy Number One. The most cruel and slanderous accusations ever made against Jesus were made by these church people. They called him a "winebibber," a "glutton," and I feel sure joined the scribes in regarding him as being possessed by "Beelzebub, . . . the prince of the devils." Similarly the harshest words spoken by Jesus were addressed to these good people. He referred to them as "hypocrites," "whited sepulchres," "blind guides," "fools." He told them that the publicans and harlots would enter the kingdom before they would. "Ye serpents, ye generation of vipers, how can ye escape the damnation of hell?" So spoke Jesus to these church people, and he spoke so to no one else. "Beware of the leaven of the Pharisees, and of the leaven of Herod," he warned his disciples. The estrangement between Jesus and the Pharisees was complete. Dr. Klausner, the learned professor of the Hebrew University at Jerusalem, truly observes: "Those we struggle with must be nearest to us; and though the struggle estranges us it is the best evidence of the affinity between the . . . combatants."

Now let us observe more specifically some of the incidents of conflict between Jesus and the Pharisees. They are numerous. The following are fairly representative. Matthew, the publican, gave a dinner for Jesus to which he invited his friends. And the Pharisees were offended. "How is it that he eateth and drinketh with publicans and sinners?" The disciples of Jesus, unlike those of John and the Phari-

18

sees, did not fast. And the Pharisees were offended. "Why do the disciples of John and of the Pharisees fast, but thy disciples fast not?" Jesus and his disciples plucked the ears of corn on the Sabbath. And the Pharisees were offended. "Behold, why do they on the sabbath day that which is not lawful?" Jesus and his disciples would eat without washing their hands. And the Pharisees were offended. "Why walk not thy disciples according to the tradition of the elders, but eat bread with unwashen hands?" asked the Pharisees. Their indignation was still further increased when on the Sabbath Day Jesus healed the man with the withered hand. It was then that "the Pharisees went forth, and straightway took counsel with the Herodians against him, how they might destroy him." They never ceased their opposition until they succeeded in destroying him, as no doubt they believed.

At first thought it might appear well-nigh incredible that such seemingly trivial matters should have aroused such intense hostility. Actually, however, the incidents though seemingly trivial were of the greatest importance in what they foreshadowed. They were attacks on the law, and the law was the center of orthodox Judaism, even as the Cross is the center of Christianity. A tiny infection on the body may be of far greater moment than the immediate area it covers; if unchecked, the poison bids fair to spread contagion through the whole system. A leak in a dyke may be only a matter of a few inches and yet, if neglected, will threaten the entire structure. Similarly, while the specific acts of Jesus in violation of the law might not seem to us of great importance, nevertheless they foreshadowed a principle which, if unchallenged, would have undermined the

19

law of Moses and so the very foundations of Pharisaic Judaism. The Pharisees, then, granting their presuppositions, were wholly justified in their resentment of Jesus' attitude and so in their attack on him.

In order to see the truth of this, we must look a little more in detail at the Pharisees' attitude toward the law as compared with that of our Lord.[4] To the Pharisees the law, the Torah, was the beginning and the end of religion. The Torah means "the teaching." It was believed to have been created before the world; it was offered by God to all the nations, but only Israel accepted it. This is why Israel believed they were the chosen people of God.[5] Not only was the law given by God, but through it God had revealed his will to man. This will as revealed by the law was complete, exhaustive, and final. To change the law therefore in the slightest measure, either by adding to it or disregarding any of its demands, was to sin against God. It was blasphemy. Listen to some of the religious leaders of the day:

"The law is holy and has been given by God." ... "Only his [Moses'] decrees are everlasting and unchangeable and unshakable, as signed by nature herself with her seal." ... Those "who deny that the law is from heaven have no part in the world to come." ... "Even if one said, 'the Torah is from God with the exception of this or that verse which Moses, not God, spake from his own mouth, ... the word of the Lord he has despised' —an irreverence which it is declared merits the extermination of that soul." ... "He who says, 'The Torah is not from God,' or even if he says, 'The whole Torah is from God with the

---

[4] The best book that I have seen on this subject is Bennett Harvie Branscomb's *Jesus and the Law of Moses.* I commend it heartily to those who may desire a more exhaustive treatment than can here be given.

[5] See Clarence Tucker Craig, *The Beginning of Christianity,* p. 42.

exception of this or that verse, which, not God, but Moses spake from his own mouth'—that soul shall be rooted up." . . . "And for this law there is no limit of days, for it is forever." [6]

Such quotations suffice to show that to the Pharisees the law as given by Moses was in its origin divine, in its scope exhaustive, in its content complete, and in its duration eternal—"it is forever." In addition to the written law the Pharisees observed also the oral law, or tradition, as it was sometimes called. The tradition partly interpreted and partly supplemented the written law. The Pharisees considered the tradition just as binding as the written law. Such then in brief was their attitude to the law, written and oral.

Jesus' attitude was different; on occasion he violated the law. And yet we must not think that he had no respect for the law or was in any sense an iconoclast. On several occasions when questioned he quoted the law as his authority. Jesus was no hotheaded revolutionary without appreciation of or respect for the heritage of his fathers. Yet it seems clear from the Gospels that unlike the Pharisees he did not regard this heritage uncritically, as though all parts of the law were of equal importance or worth. For example, he differentiated between the moral and ceremonial aspects of the law, between those teachings of Scripture or tradition which were of ethical import and those which were ethically irrelevant. It appears that Jesus regarded God as being greater than the law of Moses, and therefore believed that one might betray the will of God by giving a too slavish adherence to the minutiae of the law. "Why do ye also transgress the commandment of God by your tradition?" [7] It

[6] As quoted by Branscomb, *op. cit.*, pp. 22-23, 156, 25.
[7] Matt. 15:3.

is evident that here we confront two points of view: that of the conservative ecclesiastic who holds to tradition come what may, who mistakes the "hoary" for the "holy"; and that of a fearless prophetic spirit who, reverencing the past and its great values, yet believes that "time makes ancient good uncouth." For while Jesus regarded the law as of great importance, there were some matters he viewed as being of greater importance. Whenever strict obedience to the law militated against matters of greater moment, the law became to Jesus of secondary consideration. Let us then *in the light of the Cross* consider some of the differences in emphasis between Jesus' attitude to the law and that of the Pharisees. In so doing we shall reveal the evils which have beset ecclesiasticism from the days of the Pharisees until now. Why were the Pharisees offended?

For one thing, because Jesus put human need above the law. Whenever the law conflicted with some humane ministry, Jesus disregarded the law. God's primary law was the law of righteousness and love expressed in service to man. The ecclesiastic often sacrifices to tradition what is vitally and humanely relevant. To pluck the ears of corn or heal the man with the withered hand on the Sabbath Day was to break the law of Moses, but to fail to do either would break what our Lord must have regarded as a greater law of God, namely, service to a brother man in need. What was humanely relevant was given precedence. "The sabbath was made for man, and not man for the sabbath." The same motive explains why Jesus ate and drank with publicans and sinners. In refusing to do this, the Pharisees were adhering to a valid religious principle, namely, separateness from the world. It is a fundamental Christian principle.

Paul voices it when he says, "Come out from among them, and be ye separate, saith the Lord." But separateness to the Pharisees too often meant exclusiveness, while religion to Jesus was more than an external barrier against defilement —it was the spirit of aggressive good will to all sorts and conditions of men. "They that be whole need not a physician, but they that are sick. . . . I am not come to call the righteous, but sinners to repentance." [8] Jesus would keep himself clean by cleansing the world, and in saving others save himself. He thus was exemplifying God's supreme law, the law of love. As John Robert Seeley puts it in "Ecce Homo," "he set the first and greatest example of a life wholly governed and guided by the passion of humanity."

Again, the Pharisees were offended because Jesus by his attitude to the law showed that he regarded the inner motive or spirit of an act as of greater moment than its outward performance. This attitude inevitably brought him into conflict with the Pharisees, who, ecclesiastics that they were, placed outward conformity above inner motive. The meticulous performance of some outward act was not, in Jesus' opinion, necessarily of religious significance. Not by outward deed alone, but by inner motive was man to be judged. The Pharisees did not agree with this. For example, they washed their hands before meat. This was done in the interest not of physical but of ceremonial purity. A Jew might inadvertently have come in contact with a Gentile or with another Jew who was ceremonially unclean, or with an unclean animal, or maybe with a dead body or some part thereof. The outward act of washing his hands would, so it was thought, make him pure again. One Rabbi

[8] Matt. 9:12, 13.

23

Akiba, imprisoned, was brought water each day for washing and drinking by Rabbi Joshua. On one occasion the keeper of the prison spilled half the water in taking it to his cell. Rabbi Akiba used the remaining water for washing his hands rather than quenching his thirst, saying: "He who eats with unwashed hands perpetrates a crime that ought to be punished with death. Better for me to die of thirst than to transgress the traditions of my ancestors." [9]

"Why walk not thy disciples according to the tradition of the elders, but eat bread with unwashen hands?" Because in Jesus' view the origin of impurity was not outward but inward, and hence it could be removed only by inner transformation, a new spirit within.

Do not ye yet understand, that . . . those things which proceed out of the mouth come forth from the heart; and they defile the man? For out of the heart proceed evil thoughts, murders, adulteries, fornications, thefts, false witness, blasphemies: these are the things which defile a man: but to eat with unwashen hands defileth not a man. . . . Woe unto you, scribes and Pharisees, hypocrites! for ye make clean the outside of the cup and of the platter, but within they are full of extortion and excess. Thou blind Pharisee, cleanse first that which is within the cup and platter, that the outside of them may be clean also. . . . Ye are like unto whited sepulchres, which indeed appear beautiful outward; . . . even so ye also outwardly appear righteous unto men, but within ye are full of hypocrisy and iniquity." [10]

Religion became for the Pharisees, as the late Kemper Fullerton of Oberlin College has said, "simply right be-

[9] From A. B. Bruce, *Training of the Twelve*, p. 82.
[10] Matt. 15:17-20; 23:25-28.

haviour before God instead of being a communion of man with God in order to right behaviour."

It follows from this that to Jesus the religious life was not a level country but a country of hills and valleys. To some aspects of it he gave primary consideration, to others, secondary. The Pharisees did not do this. They had a way, as do all thoroughgoing ecclesiastics, of specializing in trivialities. To this day that is one of the evils of ecclesiasticism. "Woe unto you, scribes and Pharisees, hypocrites! for ye pay tithe of mint and anise and cummin, and have omitted the weightier matters of the law, judgment, mercy, and faith." [11] The Pharisees did not, for instance, differentiate between the ceremonial and the moral law, and at times would even put the ceremonial above the moral law. It was perhaps this perversion of values that made Jesus accuse them of cant and hypocrisy. With Jesus the emphasis was reversed. He saw men establishing right relationships with God, not through the mechanical, meticulous performance of trivial rites, but by right relationship with their fellow men. As the Jewish scholar Joseph Klausner has written, "perhaps nothing could have so aroused the opposition of Jesus toward the Pharisees as this importance attached to such trivial religious details which to the Pharisees . . . had come to be the primary elements of the religious life." The Pharisees often made ecclesiasticism the enemy of truth. They seemed incapable of distinguishing between what was primary and secondary in religion. They treated trifles as though they were serious matters, and serious matters as though they were trifles. They paid vastly more regard to the letter of the law than to the spirit of it.

[11] Matt. 23:23.

They therefore were "blind guides, which strain at a gnat, and swallow a camel." By this perverted sense of values they did not know which was the greater, "the gold, or the temple that sanctifieth the gold, ... the gift, or the altar that sanctifieth the gift." "O Jerusalem, Jerusalem, which killest the prophets"—precisely because the prophets espoused a scale of values which challenged the pretensions of the priestly class, who were the meticulous devotees of the non-essential.

Here, then, were three ways in which Jesus' emphasis differed from that of the ecclesiastics of his day: First, he put human need before the law. Second, he emphasized the inner spirit or motive of the act rather than the outward act itself. Third, he put first things first and so made the ceremonial subservient to the moral.

Such emphasis, however, inevitably led to another difference between the Master and the ecclesiastics: the religion of Jesus left room for development and growth in a way which orthodox Pharisaism did not. The door was not quite closed in Pharisaism; a little room for progress was left in the *interpretation* of the law. But for the most part in Pharisaism God had spoken the final word and had nothing more to say. Jesus, too, it appears, attached a certain finality to the law. He is quoted as having said: "For verily I say unto you, Till heaven and earth pass, one jot or one tittle shall in no wise pass from the law, till all be fulfilled." It is evident, however, that Jesus often went through the fences of legalism and won new territory for God. "He taught them as one that had authority, and not as the scribes." The scribes taught them from the book; they were authoritarians. Jesus, while he held the Scriptures in highest regard, often taught out of his own heart and experience. His God was not the God of a book only, but the living God who speaks through personality, redeemed and submissive to his righteous will. "He closed the book . . . and sat down. . . . And he began to say unto them, This day is this scripture fulfilled in your ears." [12] So Jesus came, as he said, not "to destroy the law, . . . but to fulfill" it. And to Jesus' way of thinking the law was fulfilled in a life.

God to Jesus was the God who speaks. His new messages, like new wine, could not always be confined within the old wineskins. Jesus could say to his disciples: "I have yet many things to say unto you, but ye cannot bear them now. Howbeit when he, the Spirit of truth, is come, he will guide you into all truth: . . . and he will shew you things to come." To the Pharisees such an attitude was impossible. There was nothing still "to come"; God had spoken once and for all—nothing was left to be said. We may say then that, speaking broadly, Pharisaism was a static religion, while Christ brought a dynamic religion. This statement might not be wholly true, since there was a liberal group in Pharisaism which, had they been in the majority, might have been more in sympathy with our Lord's progressive spirit and probably would not have opposed him as did the ultraconservative element who were in the majority.

This dynamic character of Jesus' teaching makes by and large one big difference between the Old Testament and the New. The Old Testament is the seed out of which the gospel has flowered; it is the foundation upon which the grand superstructure of our faith is built. Yet there is a difference between the Testaments. Is it not true that when

[12] Luke 4:20, 21.

we come into the New Testament we are in the country of pioneers? Of course this does not imply that there are no pioneers in the Old Testament; that would be very far from the truth. The prophets were trail blazers in the finest sense. Their influence on Jesus' life and ministry is too well known to be mentioned. Yet, taken as a whole, it is I think fair to say that the pioneering spirit informs the New Testament. The people who meet us there are looking not backward but forward; they are not following old paths but blazing new trails; they are not imitators but creators; they talk about making all things new. They are adventurers. This is because they were followers of Christ, who was an adventurer in the finest meaning of that word. One New Testament writer refers to him as "the pioneer . . . of faith." [13]

I do not like to apply the word "radical" to the Christ, for that word is suspect and rightly so. There are always notable exceptions, but the radical is sometimes an unbalanced person who goes off "half-cocked." He has little sense of history, slight appreciation of the past and its incomparable values. He is a hotheaded iconoclast who loves to shock people, to destroy old values just to show how smart, brave, or original he is. In short, the radical is at times terribly superficial. This is unfortunate, for the word in its derivation suggests just the opposite. *Radix*, from which it is derived, means root. The true radical, then, is the man who gets to the bottom of things. In this sense Christ was undoubtedly a radical. It may be questioned if any man ever got down in such thoroughgoing fashion to the roots of things.

[13] Heb. 12:2—Moffatt.

28

There are two ways at least in which he did this. One was, as has been suggested, in his attitude to the past, to tradition. The Pharisees were traditionalists, as are all ecclesiastics. "Thus have ye made the commandment of God of none effect by your tradition," Jesus told them. He on the contrary was a radical. He got down to the roots of things, and so in tradition distinguished between the earthen vessel and the treasure, between the letter of tradition and the spirit of it. "Ye have heard that it was said by them of old time. . . . But I say unto you . . ." That is the word not of a standpatter but of a pioneer, not of one who simply follows old paths but of one who blazes new trails into the unknown country.

But Jesus was an adventurer, too, in that he did not divorce the doctrinal from the ethical. The great difference between him and the Pharisees was not that they held one set of beliefs and he another, but rather that he was morally in earnest about these beliefs and started to live as though they were really so. For example, the idea of the universal fatherhood of God and its inevitable corollary, the brotherhood of man, was to be found on page thus and so of the prophetic writings. Jesus took this belief off the page and put it into life. He began to eat and drink with the publicans and sinners, to make friends with hated Samaritans, to see good in a Roman centurion. In a word, he began to live as if this belief in God's universal fatherhood were true. And so with all the other beliefs. Jesus took these old beliefs, the stock in trade of the conventionally religious, and infused them with a new spirit, breathed the breath of life into them until they became vital, dynamic. It was as though the Pharisees said to Jesus, "Do not take these be-

liefs seriously, for if you do they will get you into trouble."
But Jesus was an adventurer. He did take them seriously,
and they did get him into trouble—they led to his crucifixion. Conservatives do not die on crosses. You and I will
probably die *of* something. Jesus died *for* something. The
cross of Jesus is the culmination of his adventurous life, the
symbol of his greatest adventure—his adventure in sacrificial love.

So far we have seen that the conflict between Jesus and
the ecclesiastics of his day sprang from a difference in emphasis. Jesus, we have noted, was not unmindful of the
values in tradition. But there were certain considerations
he put before the law, like the primacy of human need,
the importance of inner motive, the superiority of the
moral over the ceremonial, the necessity for growth and
development. Such considerations made it imperative for
him at times to cut himself loose from a static, time-hon-
ored tradition in the interest of a greater truth. This offended the ecclesiastics.

There were, however, two other ways in which he offended them. To mention these is to reveal two of the other
great evils of ecclesiasticism from Jesus' day to this. For
one thing, he challenged them ethically. This made them
indignant. They were sticklers for the niceties of ecclesiastical practice but had omitted the weightier matters of the
law—judgment, mercy, and faith. Jesus therefore embar-
rassed the Pharisees by revealing a religion more ethically
vital than their own. This practice of waging a theological
battle over issues that are often irrelevant, and so ignoring
great ethical realities, is still a major evil of ecclesiasticism.

There were three crosses on Calvary. All three men were crucified because they were regarded as enemies of society. The fact that Jesus' cross was in the middle might suggest that he was looked upon as the greatest enemy of the three. Two of the men were crucified because they were predatory bandits, and one because he came to redeem the world. To put the matter bluntly, two men were crucified because they were too bad, and one because he was too good. You see, as Henry Sloane Coffin says, "we level up with our standards of right, and we also level down. He who is above the conscience of the community is as likely to be slain as he who is below." Good people are prone to oppose and fight not only those forces in a community which are ethically below the accepted standard but also those which are ethically above that standard. They resent not only being pulled down to a lower level but—just as stubbornly—being pushed up to a higher one. Now the religion of Jesus was admittedly on a higher level ethically than that of the scribes and Pharisees. "Except your righteousness shall exceed the righteousness of the scribes and Pharisees, ye shall in no case enter into the kingdom of heaven," Jesus once said to his disciples. But the Pharisees were no more inclined to move up to the level of Jesus than to move down to the level of the bandits, for one great evil of good people is their assumption that they are good enough. Their greatest sin is that they make the good the enemy of the better. The Pharisees were no exception. They fought those who challenged them from above no less than those who threatened them from below. Both groups were considered public enemies of society, public disturbers of the peace. And so they crucified their bandits and their saviors—the

31

bandits because they were too bad for them, the saviors because they were too good for them.

The Pharisees of course are not alone in this. The sin of persecuting or killing her betters has been one of the gross sins of the church from the martyrdom of Stephen on down through the centuries. Men like Wycliffe, Huss, Savonarola, Latimer, Tyndale, John Bunyan, George Fox, or Roger Williams tower above their misguided ecclesiastical tormentors and torturers even as Jesus towered above Caiaphas and Pilate. The thoroughgoing ecclesiastic actually becomes incapable after a while of recognizing the truth when he sees it. "If thou hadst known, even thou, at least in this thy day, the things which belong unto thy peace! *but now they are hid from thine eyes.*" [14]

We have not yet considered, however, what might be regarded as the main source of conflict between Jesus and the Pharisees: Jesus hurt their pride. Through all the centuries preceding Jesus they had had, if we may so say, a corner on the religious market. "We have Abraham to our father," they said; and we read, "The . . . Pharisees sit in Moses' seat." And loved it! as someone has suggested. They were the accredited official religious class to whom people looked for religious guidance, and they possessed the pride which usually, if not invariably, accompanies the sense of exclusive right or monopoly. And here came Jesus, this relatively unknown prophet of Nazareth, who dared to challenge them, who won people to himself by the transparent sincerity of his spirit and the unquestionable power that came to him as the loyal, obedient, and devoted Son of God. This offended the pride of the Pharisees. Pride is

[14] Luke 19:42.

perhaps the worst human sin; and ecclesiastical pride is the worst expression of pride, since to our natural conceit it adds the sanction and sanctity of God. The combination is terrific! The ecclesiastic comes in time actually to identify his own particular views and those of his group with the voice of the eternal God.

Ecclesiastical pride is still regnant in the church. It is one of the sins that are constantly crucifying the Son of God afresh. Consider our divided Protestantism. This is due no doubt to many causes, yet I venture that pride stands today as a major barrier to Protestant unity and accounts for a good deal of our ecclesiastical stubbornness, stupidity, and shortsightedness. In 1890 there were in the United States 145 denominations. Today there are 256. This is not quite as bad as it seems, since in 1936 less than one fourth of the denominations had 98 per cent of the membership. Even so, our Protestant disunity may justly be described as "ecclesiastical anarchy." No wonder Jacques Bossuet could exclaim: "Great God! Is it possible that upon the same matters and same questions, so many multiplied acts, so many divisions and different confessions of faith are necessary? . . . These variations fill us with astonishment." A well-known Japanese Christian whose English was not too fluent, speaking once in England about Christian unity, had difficulty with the word "denominations." He would say, by a slip in his English, "damnations." Was he really so far wrong? We Protestants love to sing:

> Like a mighty army
> Moves the church of God.

The Protestant church is a mighty army, but it does not move like one; rather it moves like miscellaneous groups of isolated squads, each marching with indifference and sometimes even in opposition to the others. There is no long-distance plan, no over-all strategy. The wasted effort, the duplications, the sheer appalling inefficiency resulting from the scandal of our meaningless divisions is distressing to contemplate. "The children of this world," said the Master, "are in their generation wiser than the children of light." How painfully true! If only the children of light could learn a lesson from the last war. What was the secret of victory in the last war? "Unified command" and "combined chiefs of staff." That is why the United Nations won the war—and why the divided churches of Protestantism have been giving ground before the hosts of secularism.

It must not be thought, of course, that we are pleading for Protestant uniformity. Ernest Findlay Scott in his illuminating book *The Varieties of New Testament Religion* makes it absolutely clear that from New Testament days division was involved in the very nature of Christianity. While the early Christians were all inspired by one faith, they were never slaves to one interpretation of it. A unity that destroys the differences that spring from Christian liberty of thought is not the unity we want. Paul has given us a fine picture of Christian unity in his familiar symbol of the body and its members: "Now are they many members, yet but one body"—unity in diversity. It is for that unity that I plead, and the outlook for it was probably never brighter than now. It is said that one day when Phillips Brooks was walking along the Maine shore at low tide he observed little isolated pools on the broken coast which reminded him sorrowfully of the broken-up condition of Protestantism. Later on that day, however, as he looked out from his porch, a different picture greeted him. The little separated pools were gone because the tide had come in. There is good reason today to believe that the tide is moving in on our Protestant disunity. Years ago an Indian Christian woman, when asked what she was religiously, replied, "I am an American Dutch Reformed Indian Christian!" Now she would probably say, "I am an Indian Christian," or, better still, "I am a Christian from India." With such splendid organizations as the Federal Council of the Churches of Christ in America and now the World Council of Churches, there is ground for hope. That hope will be more fully realized as Christians come to recognize that, in Walter W. Van Kirk's phrase, "it is spreading the gospel that counts, not counting sectarian noses."

When, however, one turns from Protestantism to Roman Catholicism he encounters a much more difficult situation. There is hope for unity among Protestants; there seems to be little or no hope for unity between Protestants and Roman Catholics. Ecclesiastical pride presents a vastly more formidable barrier in Roman Catholicism than in Protestantism, and that for three reasons. In the first place, Roman Catholicism unblushingly claims to be in complete possession of all the truth there is. So far as I know, no Protestant group claims a complete monopoly of religious truth. It is true that the arrogance and bigotry of some Protestant sects might seem to deny that statement, but the statement holds true. It is otherwise, however, in Roman Catholicism. For instance, as recently as December, 1945, Pope Pius made an appeal for Christian unity. The substance of it was that all Protestants should return, lock, stock, and barrel, to the Roman Catholic church, confess their sins, and be reinstated. That the Pope in this day and age should ask Protestants to repudiate some five hundred years of their history and so admit that their claims have been wholly invalid, would be amusing were it not so unspeakably tragic. For his appeal, made no doubt in good faith, shows how ecclesiasticism makes one not only insensitive to the canons of good taste but completely blind to the realities of a given situation. One wonders whether in making such an appeal, in which he demands the one hundred per cent capitulation of Protestants and offers not the slightest concession in return except a willingness to receive the repentant sinners—one wonders if it even occurs to him that such an appeal would seem to the average Protestant as nothing more than an almost incredible expression of ecclesiastical arrogance. It is worth while to quote in this connection the words of Walter W. Van Kirk in his recent book, *A Christian Global Strategy*:

Any communion of religious worshipers that seeks to establish itself as the exclusive witness to the Christian faith is gravely endangering the larger interests of the Kingdom of God upon earth. Any government that yields to the pressure of one branch of the church to the disadvantage and threatened extinction of any other branch should be made to account for such action before the bar of world public opinion.

... Ecclesiastical monopolies are insufferable, be they Roman Catholic, Protestant or Orthodox. To hold that the God of the Christians has elected to reveal himself solely and exclusively through the instrumentalities of a particular religious institution is blasphemy.[15]

[15] Willett, Clark & Co., pp. 117-18.

The ecclesiastical monopoly of Roman Catholicism expresses itself not just in words but in deeds, too. Take for example the matter of religious freedom. It is no secret at all that the Roman Catholic hierarchy preaches religious freedom in those countries in which Roman Catholics are in the minority but fails to practice it in those lands where they are in the majority. Indeed, it is a fact that in such countries non-Roman Christians have been maligned and even persecuted. This is arrogance in action. In the early history of Protestantism similar conditions have existed. Reinhold Niebuhr writes in *The Nature and Destiny of Man*: "In the long history of religious controversy in England from the reign of Elizabeth to that of Cromwell, Presbyterianism pursued a policy very similar to that of Catholicism. It pled for liberty of conscience when it was itself in danger of persecution; and threatened all other denominations with suppression when it had the authority to do so." There is, however, this big difference: The basic ideas of democracy and freedom which inhere in Protestantism constantly militate against such moral inconsistency, while the spirit of authoritarianism, if not religious totalitarianism, which informs Roman Catholicism makes such actions ecclesiastically consistent and so tends to obscure their moral incongruity.

The second reason why ecclesiasticism is more formidable a foe in Roman Catholicism than in Protestantism is that for all intents and purposes Roman Catholicism identifies the church with the kingdom of God. Protestants believe that the church is divinely instituted and fulfills a divine function. But they do not identify it with the absolute and eternal truth. On the contrary, they constantly criticize and evaluate the institutional aspects of the church's life in the light of the kingdom, which transcends the church and is the great end for which the church performs its ministry. Richard Niebuhr penetratingly remarks that the average American Protestant is more interested in the kingdom of God than in the church as such. Not so, however, in Roman Catholicism. Here the church is the kingdom. It is not a means to an end but an end in itself. In order to promote its prestige and its power the hierarchy resorts to policies and practices which one would hardly expect of an institution that calls itself Christian. For instance, the Roman Catholic hierarchy has given its blessing to gambling, provided the winnings go to the church! Such a divorce between theology and morality, religion and ethics, is appalling to contemplate. Should any such evil be countenanced today by a Protestant church, there would be a thousand voices within the church that in the light of God's eternal kingdom would bring the church to judgment. But there are no such voices within Roman Catholicism, for there is no such eternal truth in the light of which the Roman Catholic church is judged. The church is the truth.

The third reason why ecclesiasticism is more of a problem in the Roman Catholic church is because here it is augmented by clericalism. President John Mackay of Princeton, whose years in South America make him an authority on this subject, writes: "Clericalism is the pursuit of political power by a religious hierarchy, carried on by secular methods and for purposes of social domination." He adds, in words which should give all loyal Americans,

Roman Catholic and Protestant alike, food for thought: "It is painful to contemplate the sinister emergence of this phenomenon for the first time in American history. It will work its own disaster in Anglo-Saxon North America as it has already done in Iberian South America, but its onward march may leave much wreckage behind it." [16]

It is for these reasons that Protestant ecclesiasticism, while bad enough in all conscience, is not so great an obstacle to Christian fellowship as Roman Catholic ecclesiasticism. In Protestantism unity is by no means to be despaired of, though the road may be long and progress slow. There is, however, little or no hope for unity between Roman Catholics and Protestants unless the hierarchy abandons its extravagant and, as it seems to me, utterly indefensible position. Only the grace of God will accomplish that.

It must not be thought for a moment that in speaking thus of the evils of ecclesiasticism I am condemning institutionalized Christianity. There are those who in seeking to cure the evils of ecclesiasticism advocate a Christianity sans church, sans dogmas, sans doctrines. No such Christianity has ever existed or could exist. No such Christianity could endure. Occasionally one meets a person who when presented with the claims of the church replies, "I don't need the church; I have my own religion"; or, "My religion is the Golden Rule." No doubt such good people take themselves quite seriously, but it would be too bad for us to take them seriously. Actually, such statements are childish and naïve in the extreme, betraying

[16] Editorial, *Theology Today,* January, 1946.

a complete innocence of the nature and purpose of the Christian religion.

As a matter of fact, had it not been for the church, the institution, we should never even have heard of Christ, let alone the Golden Rule. It was in the fellowship of the church that Christian faith was born. It was due to the fellowship of the church that Christian faith was formulated and the Bible came into being. It was by the fellowship of the church that Christian faith was nurtured and propagated through the darkest days of its history. A churchless Christianity is an anachronism, and even if it existed would bear no resemblance to the historic faith which we profess. A disembodied Christianity will not function in this world of flesh and blood—especially in this age in which paganism presents itself not as abstract ethical principles but as dynamic, passionate movements like communism and fascism, which are in their ultimate nature vigorous faiths. To meet the enemies of Christ today singlehanded with any such slogan as "I have my own religion" is to enter an unequal struggle the outcome of which is a foregone conclusion. The evils of ecclesiasticism can be cured without killing the patient.

It is impossible within brief limits to suggest the cure, and yet when it is found I fancy it will move in the direction of a few basic principles. The evils of ecclesiasticism will be overcome as the church realizes that it is not an end itself but a means to an end beyond itself, and so will not identify the treasure with the earthen vessel; as the church sees clearly that no one ecclesiastical formula or practice adequately contains, let alone exhausts, the Christian truth; as the church places the Christian

40

ideal of love as expressed in the Golden Rule or the thirteenth chapter of First Corinthians above the ecclesiastical ideal which so often makes the law of love "of none effect"; as the church follows more courageously the "Spirit of truth" who Jesus said will "guide you into all truth" and "will shew you things to come"; as the church realizes more fully the meaning of the Cross, that symbol of brave, sacrificial, spiritual and ethical pioneering.

That Cross was erected largely because Jesus disregarded and even attacked some of the outworn ecclesiastical practices of his day and so rescued the treasure from the earthen vessel which had become inadequate and was imperiling its life. The fearless courage and self-effacing love of that cross may yet save the church from the evils of ecclesiasticism.

II

Privilege: *The Sadducees*

THE SADDUCEES were religious secularists, "ecclesiastical men of the world." Though they were more conservative in their religious beliefs than the Pharisees, yet their primary interest was not religious but secular. It is true that sometimes the ultraconservative in religion is much more concerned about the quieting effect of religion on society in general than he is in facing its ethical challenge. He acts on the assumption that "the old-time religion," which he mistakenly supposes bears no relation to economics, politics, or any social problem, will preserve the *status quo* and so his own favored position. At any rate, the Sadducees, while quite orthodox, more so than the Pharisees, had little or no interest in religion. They were astute politicians, worldly wise, concerned about prestige and preference.

Perhaps the Sadducees might be most aptly described by the word "privilege." Along with the merchants, the landed proprietors and the rich financiers, they made up the aristocracy. This position of privilege grew largely from the fact that they had come to terms with Rome. The Jews in their attitude to Roman rule may be divided into three groups. There were the Zealots, hotheaded revolutionaries, who favored insurrection and often indeed attempted it. Then there were those who, although cognizant of the folly and hopelessness of resistance, were yet inwardly incensed at their servitude to an alien power.

"They knew that resistance was a physical impossibility and only invited complete destruction and devastation. They did not love Rome because they could not fight; they hated her the more. Their non-resistance was with a glowing eye and a heart full of hate, but with an arm that did not dare to strike." [1]

There was, however, a third group, represented by the Sadducees. Not only were they nonresistant but they would not have resisted if they could have. The Sadducees might well have argued: Why worry about submission to a foreign power if by co-operating with that power you better your position? Any change in the national situation might change your personal situation—for the worse. "The Romans shall come and take away . . . our place." That was the place of privilege. The Sadducees knew which side their bread was buttered on. Practical politicians that they were, they were content to let well enough alone. There was something of the "Quisling" in them. They were collaborationists. This may explain why they feared a messianic movement led by Jesus and so condemned him for claiming to be the Messiah. The fact that, as Joseph Klausner says, "no indubitably Sadducean document survives in Judaism" is proof enough that the Sadducees had no deep roots in the nation's life. Indeed, after the destruction of Jerusalem they disappeared entirely from history. During Jesus' lifetime, however, they were very much in evidence, occupying as they did the seats of privilege.

It was the economic issue which first brought these privileged folk into direct conflict with the Master. To be

[1] Vladimir G. Simkhovitch, *Toward the Understanding of Jesus*, p. 45.

sure, they differed with him religiously, specifically over the question of the resurrection. Since, however, the Sadducees were not primarily interested in religious matters, they would not have opposed him had he not made a direct attack on their economic privilege. This Jesus was moved to do when, during the last week of his life, he drove the money changers out of the temple. The Sadducees had charge of the temple; they were the priestly class. Their temple trading provided a most lucrative source of wealth. It has been estimated that some twenty thousand priests ministered in the temple. Some of them, though serving for only a few days in any given year, would exact a full year's pay. The populace had to pay not only Roman taxes but priestly taxes in addition. It has also been estimated that forty per cent of the average income of the people was taken away in taxes. Indeed, the high priests controlled not only the taxes but the whole temple market.

The income of the temple market derived from two sources. One was the sale of doves and lambs without blemish—fit for sacrifice. From far and wide during the Passover season the pilgrims would come to Jerusalem to make sacrifices in the temple. But it was not convenient for them to bring their sacrificial doves or lambs with them. The Sadducean priests had country estates where animals to be sacrificed in the temple were raised. This was ostensibly for the convenience of the pilgrims, but in reality it was a most lucrative means of gain, since they charged exorbitant prices for these animals which could be obtained nowhere else. That was one source of their wealth.

And there was another. Every Passover pilgrim coming to Jerusalem had to pay a temple tax. The pilgrims—from neighboring lands like Persia, Syria, Egypt, Greece, Rome—were not permitted to pay this tax in the coins of the countries from which they came, because such coins had engraved on them the heads of kings or emperors, gods or goddesses. To take these into the temple looked too much like worshiping a graven image. All these coins then had to be exchanged for temple shekels; hence the tables of the money changers. But in making the exchange the Sadducean priests charged exorbitant rates, so that here again they increased their income. Indeed, it has been estimated that during the few days leading up to the Passover the money changers would make a profit of between forty and fifty thousand dollars.[2]

It was this sort of business that was going on in the temple when Jesus came to Jerusalem during the last week of his life. "And Jesus went into the temple, and began to cast out them that sold and bought in the temple, and overthrew the tables of the moneychangers, and the seats of them that sold doves. . . . And he taught, saying unto them, Is it not written, My house shall be called of all nations the house of prayer? but ye have made it a den of thieves." [3] The Sadducees were not greatly disturbed over Jesus' religious views. When, however, he dared to challenge their shady economic practices, he stepped on their toes. As Halford E. Luccock puts it, "Jesus was not crucified for saying, 'Consider the lilies of the field, how

[2] Basil Mathews, *Life of Jesus*, p. 375.
[3] Mark 11:15, 17.

they grow'; what got him into trouble was saying, 'Consider the thieves of the Temple, how they steal.'" For no sooner had Jesus attacked them than "the . . . chief priests heard it, and sought how they might destroy him." As the late Canon Streeter once wrote, "he stirred up a hornets' nest, and the hornets stung." So economic privilege helped to crucify Jesus.

There are at least three other instances in the New Testament in which economic privilege is seen in opposition to the truth. They are quite familiar and yet it may not be inappropriate to mention them. One is found in the Gospel of Mark. Jesus met a man possessed of demons. We should not thus describe his ailment. When Jesus inquired his name, he said, "My name is Legion: for we are many." "Multiple selves" might be our way of saying that today. Jesus healed the demoniac, and we are told that the evil spirits, being cast out, went into a herd of swine that ran violently down a steep place and into the sea. They were drowned. The citizens on hearing what had happened were not so much impressed that a man was saved as they were disturbed that their pigs were lost. "And they began to pray him to depart out of their coasts." They thought more of their pigs than they did of people.

Another incident is recorded in the book of Acts. Paul and Silas met a young woman at Philippi who is described as "possessed with a spirit of divination . . . which brought her masters much gain by soothsaying." She was converted by Paul, and when a truly divine power got hold of her, she lost her spirit of divination. "And when her masters saw that the hope of their gains was gone, they caught Paul

46

and Silas, and drew them into the marketplace unto the rulers, . . . saying, These men . . . do exceedingly trouble our city, and teach customs, which are not lawful for us to receive. . . . And when they had laid many stripes upon them, they cast them into prison." [4] This highly solicitous regard for "our city" was of course a red herring. The plain truth is that these Romans, too, thought more of their money than they did of a human being.

The third incident, also from the book of Acts, occurred at Ephesus. Here stood the shrine of Diana, the pagan goddess. One Demetrius, a silversmith, plied a lucrative trade by making little silver shrines of Diana, which found a ready market. Paul preached against such paganism. Demetrius called together his fellow craftsmen and said, "Sirs, ye know that by this craft we have our wealth." It is easy to see that the rest of his speech, in which he praises the temple and the great Diana, was really superfluous:

Moreover ye see and hear, that not alone at Ephesus, but almost throughout all Asia, this Paul hath persuaded and turned away much people, saying that they be no gods, which are made with hands: so that not only this our craft is in danger to be set at nought; but also that the temple of the great goddess Diana should be despised, and her magnificence should be destroyed, whom all Asia and the world worshippeth. And when they heard these sayings, they were full of wrath, and cried out, saying, Great is Diana of the Ephesians.[5]

The great Diana never seemed so great as when her loss of prestige threatened the source of the silversmith's fraud-

[4] Acts 16:19-21, 23.
[5] Acts 19:26-28.

ulent business. Here again, if truth be told, the Ephesians preferred profits to people.

In each of these instances the conflict between economic privilege and the gospel is the same. The conflict always involves the worth of personality. In the case of the Sadducees, the pilgrims were fleeced. The people of Gadara regarded their vested interests as of more value than human life. The owners of the Philippian girl would rather exploit her abnormality than see her whole. The silversmiths at Ephesus resented and resisted the liberating of the public by the preaching of the truth, for they wanted a market for their little tin gods, which, though made of silver, were tin gods just the same.

Not alone in the New Testament, however, does one find such instances as these. Our own secular history abounds in them. Take slavery, for example. During an antislavery meeting in New York City, a northern merchant called out to Mr. May, the philanthropist: "Mr. May, we are not such fools as not to know that slavery is a great evil, a great wrong. . . . A great portion of the property of the Southerners is invested under its sanction; and the business of the North, as well as the South, has become adjusted to it. . . . We cannot afford, sir, to let you and your associates succeed in your endeavor to overthrow slavery." [6] At least, this man was honest and far more straightforward than the pious folk who carried on the nefarious slave trade behind a façade of misused Scripture texts.

Or consider the missionary movement. In 1789, when William Carey announced his plan to go as a missionary

[6] From Harry Emerson Fosdick, *The Meaning of Service*, pp. 174-75.

to India, he was bitterly opposed by the East India Company. The directors assembled and issued the following proclamation: "The sending out of missionaries into our Eastern possessions is the maddest, most extravagant, most costly, most indefensible project which has ever been suffered by a moon-struck fanatic. Such a scheme is pernicious, imprudent, useless, harmful, dangerous, profitless, fantastic. It strikes against all reason and sound policy. It brings the peace and safety of our possessions in peril." [7] The last sentence is the really important one; the rest was just by way of introduction.

Similar incidents out of our own day and generation could be cited to show that from the days of the Sadducees until now the safeguarding of economic privilege has endangered and often thwarted the progress of man. There can be no doubt that some of the most serious abuses in our civilization spring from this source. It may not be an exaggeration to say that truth is betrayed and crucified today more by money than by any other single force. "The love of money," said Paul, "is the root of all evil." Not *money*, mark you, which can be the source of endless good, but the *love* of money. In view of this, it is not surprising that the Master had so much to say about money. As a matter of fact, it is probably true that Jesus said more about money than about any other single subject.

In his ministry Jesus dealt with the economically privileged as well as with the underprivileged. In men like Nicodemus, the rich young ruler, the Roman centurion, Zacchaeus, he was dealing with the more highly favored,

[7] From Stanley High, *The Church in Politics,* p. 105.

while the woman of Samaria, the Syrophoenician woman, the lepers, the blind and the lame, represent the less fortunate to whom he ministered. It has often been said that Jesus was the friend of the underprivileged. That is true. This does not mean, however, that he was not a friend of the privileged. He was. He was interested in people as people. Some of his most forceful utterances were made against the wealthy, but not, I think, because they were wealthy but because they allowed their wealth to make them callous and self-centered and so to build a barrier between themselves and their fellow men. Jesus said it was easier for a camel to go through the eye of a needle than for such men to enter into the kingdom of God. In that kingdom not temporal positions but timeless values come first. It seems to me that any attempt to make Jesus the exclusive champion of any one race, class, or nation is doomed to failure.

While this is so, yet no one can read the New Testament without realizing that the poor, the sick, the neglected—in short, the underprivileged—occupied the greater part of Jesus' time and thought. This was because their need was greater. "They that are whole have no need of the physician, but they that are sick." So he preached and so he practiced. Like a physician, he must attend first to the sick. In doing so the physician bears no grudge against the well.

The opposition to truth from the abuse of economic privilege runs through the Bible like the ever-recurring theme of a symphony. We have noted illustrations from the New Testament and from contemporary life, but we cannot forget that the roots go back into the Old Testament.

Some of the most piercing and uncompromising insights of that book center around the abuse of economic privilege. How the prophets faced that issue! There was Micah, for instance, the prophet of the poor. He saw that wealth, instead of bringing the awareness of obligation, only served as an incentive to greater covetousness and greed. The reformers themselves needed reforming, since they, too, had become infected with greed.

> Leaders of Jacob, listen to this,
> you judges over the house of Israel,
> who spurn at justice and twist equity,
> who build your Sion up with bloodshed
> and Jerusalem on crime,
> judges passing verdicts for a bribe,
> priests pattering oracles for pay,
> prophets divining for money,
> and all the while relying on the Eternal,
> saying, "Surely the Eternal is among us;
> no evil can befall us!"
> Therefore on your account
> shall Sion be ploughed up like a field,
> Jerusalem shall become a heap of ruins.[8]

In like manner, Amos. He lived in a time when the economically privileged were enjoying a period of great prosperity while the underprivileged suffered and starved. "There were plenty of palaces and also plenty of hovels," as Kyle M. Yates puts it. There were feasting and banqueting, winter houses and summer houses, ornately decorated and furnished in elegant style; but all this luxury existed in the midst of appalling human need. Privilege had be-

[8] Mic. 3:9-12—Moffatt.

come a wall too high to be seen over, too thick to be broken through. Yes, there was religion, too, but it was formal and ecclesiastical. It was the kind of religion I observed in Rome many years ago, where beautiful churches with their costly jewels and bedecked priests looked out upon the most shocking scenes of squalor and poverty. I suppose this seemed more striking in Rome than similar scenes in our own country because there the churches are so singularly ornate.

Such was the situation long ago when Amos, this man of God, appeared. His words come ringing down the centuries: "They sold the righteous for silver, and the poor for a pair of shoes. . . . Woe to them that are at ease in Zion, . . . that lie upon beds of ivory, and stretch themselves upon their couches, and eat the lambs out of the flock, and the calves out of the midst of the stall; . . . but they are not grieved for the affliction of Joseph." [9] Dr. Moffatt translates that last sentence:

> With never a single thought
> for the bleeding wounds of the nation.

No wonder the formal religionist Amaziah ordered this fearless prophet to leave: "Visionary, be gone! Get thee off to the land of Judah." It is a favorite practice of the privileged to regard as visionary or impractical whoever or whatever comes too close for comfort. To get rid of the prophet, however, was not to be rid of the truth the prophet boldly proclaimed—namely, the danger of privilege without responsibility: "Woe to them that are at ease

[9] Amos 2:6b; 6:1-6.

in Zion." To be at ease in the place of privilege and take it for granted is to adopt an attitude that is religiously indefensible and fraught with danger. So Amos represents God as saying: "You only have I known of all the families of the earth: *therefore* I will punish you for all your iniquities."

With such a heritage as that of the prophets, it is not to be wondered at that the Master himself spoke such strong words about the economically privileged. He saw selfishness as the great peril of the economically privileged, who, figuratively speaking, put up a sign: "Private Property—Keep Out—No Trespassing." Consider his story of Dives and Lazarus. Dives, who fared sumptuously, had allowed his privileged position to make him so self-centered that he could not see even as far as his gate, where sat Lazarus, a symbol of stark poverty and need. Upon such selfish indifference Jesus pronounced unqualified condemnation. Of similar import is the story of the man who pulled down his barns and built greater. As we read this rich man's soliloquy, in every sentence we run across the personal pronouns "I" or "me"; we look in vain for "you" or "our." His bigger barns, instead of resulting in a greater sense of responsibility, a wider sympathy, a larger social concern, only created a bigger and more pampered ego. Jesus' antidote for the selfishness which invariably affects the privileged was service and some adequate sense of social responsibility. He insisted that privilege was not a luxury to be enjoyed but an obligation to be fulfilled. "Unto whomsoever much is given, of him shall be much required" was his inescapable principle of Christian morality. In his view, privilege without a corresponding sense of responsibility was immoral and indefensible. It is not surprising, therefore, that there were few evils he condemned more relentlessly than self-centered, self-indulgent living. Instead of making privilege a wall behind which one lives in seedy selfishness, Jesus taught that it should be a bridge over which one passes to the responsibilities and obligations which, from a Christian point of view, are the inevitable concomitants of privilege. He warned against covetousness and the danger of laying up treasure upon earth, the difficulty of serving God and mammon; but he did more than warn about this. He went into the temple and attacked the greedy Sadducees. Sir William Ramsey spoke truly when he said that the most sensitive part of civilized man is his pocket. That was true of the Sadducees. They were totally unconcerned about, even unaware of, the gross moral evils which their temple trading produced, yet were violently aroused when the Master threatened the source of their ill-gotten wealth. As Amaziah said to Amos, so said Caiaphas to Jesus: "Visionary, be gone!" Only he sent him not to Judah but to a cross. Economic greed helped to crucify Jesus.

The economically privileged, to be sure, have no monopoly on selfishness. Speaking from my own experience and observation, I know that one may be quite as selfish with relatively little as with relatively much. All of us living in this privileged land during this period of the world's terrific agony, when millions face starvation, would do well to take to heart an editorial written in the New York *Times* before America entered the second World War. It runs in part as follows:

Let us not be thankful because other people are cold and we are not, because others are sick and hungry and we are not. . . . Let us be thankful, but not in that spirit. . . . Let us be thankful with the thankfulness of those who cannot enjoy safety till they have done what they can to those in peril. . . . Let us be thankful because we can believe that those who hunger, who sorrow, who suffer, who die while we feast, are earning for this heartbroken earth a happier tomorrow. . . . Let us be thankful, but not complacent.[10]

Economic considerations, however, do not wholly exhaust the meaning of privilege. Too often are we wont to think that they do. As a matter of fact, a man may be privileged not only economically but intellectually, racially, socially, or religiously as well. The Sadducees were privileged folk in this larger sense also. Their resentment and antagonism to Jesus sprang not only from the fact that in cleansing the temple he interfered with their business but also from the fact that he dared to interfere with *them*. Aristocratic folk that they were, they were used to having their own way. They were accustomed to give orders, not take them. Both their position and prestige made them people of authority. Now came this relatively unknown prophet who presumed to challenge their authority, not only in his own name but in the name of the God over whose temple they presided. "By what authority doest thou these things? and who gave thee this authority?" asked the chief priests.

The wider nature of privilege is revealed interestingly enough in Mary's Magnificat, which George Bernard Shaw, rightly or wrongly, calls "the most revolutionary song that

[10] Nov. 21, 1940.

has ever been written in the history of Europe." Recall some of the phrases: "He hath scattered the proud in the imagination of their hearts"—the socially privileged. "He hath put down the mighty from their seats, and exalted them of low degree"—the racially or politically privileged. "He hath filled the hungry with good things; and the rich he hath sent empty away"—the economically privileged. This song was really prophetic, for Jesus saw privilege, whatever its nature, leading men into positions of selfishness and pride rather than of responsibility and obligation. Consider for example his parable of the wicked husbandmen. This may be taken as an instance of racial, religious, or national privilege. (In orthodox Judaism race, religion, and nation were a trinity not easily separated.) In this parable Jesus compares Israel to a vineyard. With great care the householder tended the vineyard. It was "hedged about"; it had a "wine-press" and a "tower." In short, the householder made every provision that the vineyard might "bring forth abundantly." So selfish, however, were these husbandmen that they not only failed to make any return to the absent householder for the privileges of the vineyard, but ill-treated those who were sent to them. Their selfishness reached its peak when finally the householder sent his son. In their greed they did not regard the son but only his inheritance. "This is the heir: come, let us kill him," they cried, "and let us seize on his inheritance." The verdict of the Master was that the householder would "miserably destroy those wicked men," and "let out his vineyard unto other husbandmen." Privilege selfishly abused invariably brings its own retribution.

John the Baptist had uttered a similar warning to those

who hid behind racial or national privileges: "Begin not to say within yourselves, We have Abraham to our father: for I say unto you, That God is able of these stones to raise up children unto Abraham. And now also the axe is laid unto the root of the trees: every tree therefore which bringeth not forth good fruit is hewn down, and cast into the fire." [11]

The Master was just as positive in his disapproval of the religiously privileged who boasted of their righteousness and used it as an occasion for pride and self-glorification. Consider in this connection his story of the Pharisee and the publican. We are considering the Pharisee now not as a Pharisee but simply as a symbol of religious privilege. There was unquestionably something deliberate in Jesus' choice of these two men who were poles apart in their prestige. The Pharisee, religiously speaking, was on top of the pile, the publican at the bottom. Deliberate, too, was the fact that he presents these two men at prayer. Why at prayer? Because in the presence of God the differences and distinctions which loom so large in our eyes disappear. In God's presence the Pharisee would not need to feel too proud of the fact that he was a Pharisee, nor the publican to cringe at his lack of prestige, since God would see neither Pharisee nor publican, privileged nor underprivileged, but only two men at prayer. The kind of prayer, moreover, that these men voiced indicated the kind of men that they were. "The Pharisee stood and prayed thus with himself." Note that "with himself." That, too, I fancy was deliberate. His prayer was not dialogue, as all genuine prayer aims to be, but soliloquy. "God, I

[11] Luke 3:8-9.

thank thee, that I am not as other men are." There was selfishness in his spirit, but no sympathy, haughtiness but no humility, pride but no penitence. No wonder he prayed "with himself"! "And the publican . . . would not lift up so much as his eyes unto heaven, but smote upon his breast, saying, God be merciful to me a sinner."

Now this prayer, "God, I thank thee that I am not as other men are," is a quite understandable prayer for a privileged person to make. It is, however, *in the light of the Cross* a wholly unchristian prayer. Let us see why. For one thing, it is based on a wrong assumption. Any man who allows privilege so to separate him from his fellows as to say, "God, I thank thee that I am not as other men are," is giving the Almighty false information. He knows better. That there are real differences between us, there can be no doubt at all. These differences, however, should never be allowed to conceal the underlying stuff of our common humanity. Cultural differences can be and are constantly being changed. This is the assumption that undergirds our entire missionary endeavor. In any event, the truly good man never allows the difference between himself and others to set him on a pedestal of self-righteous pride. The friend of God must always be the friend of man. When the good man becomes so conceited about his goodness that he begins to thank God that he is not like other men, then the goodness which should be a leaven permeating the lump loses its vitality.

For there is always an unstudied and unconscious element in real goodness, as there is in real greatness. This is the difference between the truly great and the near great. A truly great man is rarely conscious of his greatness, for the truly great man knows that only God is great. No more is a truly good man aware of his goodness, since the better he is the more conscious he becomes of his shortcomings. It was not false modesty that made Paul refer to himself as the chief of sinners, "least of the apostles," and "less than the least of all saints." And astonishingly enough, it was the Master who said: "Why callest thou me good? There is none good but one, that is, God." When we begin to feel proud of our goodness and to take it seriously, we may be reasonably sure that we are slipping spiritually.

This assumption that we are not as other men is responsible for two of the greatest evils of our age, racialism and nationalism. Both of these evils derive from the fact that we allow real though relatively superficial differences to becloud, if not betray, our elemental interdependencies, frailties, and sins. Both of these evils rest on false pride. They assume that our race or our nation is fundamentally and basically so different from some other—and strangely enough, by "different" we invariably mean "superior"—that we cannot meet on a plane of brotherhood, understanding, and good will. This delusion is in all our hearts. In Germany and Japan it went to its logical and therefore absurd and terrifying lengths in the arrogance of Aryan superiority and the fanaticism of Japanese nationalism. As we condemn Germany and Japan, however, for their racial and national bigotry, I can imagine the Master saying to us: "He that is without sin among you, let him first cast a stone."

For this sin of self-righteous pride which so constantly imperils the privileged, Christianity's antidote is a frank recognition of our debtorship. "What hast thou that thou didst not receive?" "Every good gift and every perfect gift is from above, and cometh down from the Father." "By grace are ye saved through faith; and that not of yourselves: it is the gift of God." "Unto one he *gave* five talents." "We are debtors," said Paul. The privileged sometimes forget this, so that when the privileged give thanks the thanks are likely to be a species of self-congratulation. The privileged naïvely assume that their favored position has been won solely by themselves. Because it is difficult for the privileged to be genuinely grateful, it is difficult for them to be genuinely humble, since humility is a concomitant of gratitude. Humility springs from gratitude, and gratitude from a realization that we receive vastly more than we deserve or merit. "Whosoever of you will be the chiefest, shall be servant of all."

This lesson needs desperately to be learned now by the privileged nations. The danger of the world today comes not from the weak but from the strong, not from the "have-nots" but from those who have. If the big nations could only now try to be big not just in power or in wealth but in their sense of responsibility and obligation, their desire for justice and fair play, then our future would be bright indeed. "He hath put down the mighty from their seats," sang Mary. You and I know or know of individuals among the most privileged in the world, whose gracious and humble spirits prove the truth of this statement. Christ has put down many mighty from their seats, not by a forcible, external revolution, but by the change wrought by his spirit within them. If only that could happen again to some of the mighty among the nations today! For is not this putting of the sense of obligation in the heart of the privileged the key to the rebuilding of this broken world?

What else do we need? Do we need brains? We have brains. A generation that can produce a B-29 bomber, a V-2 rocket bomb, to say nothing of the atomic bomb, has brains enough to devise the blueprint of a better world. But knowledge is not the only, nor even the first, requirement. If brains were the sole necessity for bringing us out of the woods, we should long since have been in the clear. Since knowledge, however, could not keep mankind out of the second World War, it most certainly will not of itself solve the bewildering problems that follow in its wake. More than knowledge, we need a new spirit. Not the spirit of self-righteous pride which makes us thank God that we are not as other men, but the spirit of penitence and humility. We need not only knowledge but wisdom, "the wisdom that is from above," which "is first pure, then peaceable." That wisdom comes to us not only from the teachings of Jesus but from his life, in which his teachings come to glorious flower.

It was of this life that Paul wrote when he said: "Treat one another with the same spirit as you experience in Christ Jesus. Though he was divine by nature, he did not snatch at equality with God, but emptied himself by taking the nature of a servant; born in human guise and appearing in human form, he humbly stooped in his obedience even to die, and to die upon the cross." [12] There is a profound insight here and, however we may explain it, a true one. The insight is that in being born as a man

[12] Phil. 2:5-8—Moffatt (2nd ed., 1913).

61

Christ relinquished a place of privilege. Equality with God was not a thing to be snatched and enjoyed selfishly, as though it were a luxury. Rather the proof that he was divine was his willingness to become human, bear our griefs, carry our sorrows, and be made in all points like unto his brethren. "If thou be Christ, save thyself." "Save thyself, and come down from the cross." It was precisely because he was the Son of God that he would not. "He saved others; himself he cannot save" was the taunt his enemies hurled at him. So stupid were they that they could not see that in their very taunt lay a triumphant truth. For in this relinquishing of his own personal rights and privileges for the redemption of man from sin and death is found one sure proof of Christ's divinity.

Indeed, herein lies one of the astounding truths of the Incarnation, namely, that not even the eternal God revels selfishly in privilege but comes in Christ to share with man his abounding redemptive love, his grace and graciousness. The infinite God dwells with finite man, and bears the disgrace, suffering, and death of a cross to prove that privilege means obligation. To live in selfishness or pride as though privilege were a luxury is to sin against the very nature of reality—that is, to sin against God.

Christ, then, is our Saviour from the perils of privilege, whatever their nature. Let the economically privileged think of him, who came not to be ministered unto but to minister and to give his life, and be delivered from greed and selfish indifference. Let the racially privileged think of him, who transcended the racial barriers of his day as naturally as the rays of the sun transcend our physical barriers, and remember his words: "For one is your Master, even Christ; and all ye are brethren." Let the intellectually privileged think of him, the wisdom of God, and be delivered from intellectual snobbery. For "the foolishness of God is wiser than men." Let the religiously privileged think of him, the fairest of ten thousand, "full of grace and truth," in whose presence our best seems poor indeed, and be freed from self-righteous pride and hypocrisy.

Jeremiah, though he spoke long ago, still speaks to our condition. You will remember his timeless words: "Let not the wise man glory in his wisdom, neither let the mighty man glory in his might, let not the rich man glory in his riches: but let him that glorieth glory in this, that he understandeth and knoweth me, that I am the Lord which exercise lovingkindness, judgment, and righteousness, in the earth: for in these things I delight, saith the Lord." [13]

To appropriate that truth, a truth which the Cross supremely teaches, is to find the key to the building of a new world. For only new men can build a new world, and only a new spirit can make men new. "Not by might, nor by power, but by my spirit, saith the Lord of hosts." It was to reveal and impart that spirit that Jesus went to his Cross.

[13] Jer. 9:23-24.

III

Nationalism: *Judas*

NATIONALISM played a major role in the crucifixion of Jesus. He was crucified because his ideas of the kingdom of God—a kingdom which he conceived as being universal—came into head-on collision with his contemporaries' conception of that kingdom, which was essentially nationalistic. The individual during Passion Week through whom the disappointed hopes of Israel found expression was Judas Iscariot.

For fear that the development of this theme should seem overly critical of nationalism, let me say at the outset that I am not condemning it wholesale. The evolution of society from the family to the clan, to the tribe, and then to the nation, was evolution in the right direction. Nationalism has contributed much to the life of civilized man. Moreover, I am not suggesting that nation states should be abolished. The kingdom of God of which Jesus spoke does not necessitate the abolition of nations. On the contrary, Jesus predicted that peoples would "come from the east, and from the west, and from the north, and from the south," each presumably bringing his own unique contribution. So, too, the seer of Revelation, in speaking of the New Jerusalem, writes, "And they shall bring the glory and honour of the nations into it."

Nationalism, however, is a sort of fetish with us and so has become one of the most formidable obstacles to

64

the progress of man and perhaps the greatest single threat to his survival. It is certainly one of Christianity's greatest rivals. It has been called "man's other religion." It is said that two thirds of the human race are devotees of the religion of nationalism. This rivalry is of long standing; indeed, it goes back to the first century. It is suggestive that no sooner was Jesus born than Herod, representative of imperial Rome, tried to kill him. He had heard that one was born who was to become king of the Jews. In an effort to destroy this potential king he ordered the slaughter of many innocent Hebrew children, a fate which the boy Jesus escaped by the flight into Egypt. If nationalism threatened him during the first days of his life, it caught up with him during his last days. The charge brought against him before Pilate was: "We found this fellow perverting the nation, and forbidding to give tribute to Caesar, saying that he himself is Christ a King." Upon his cross was inscribed in Hebrew, Greek, and Latin, "THE KING OF THE JEWS." So we might say that nationalism followed Jesus from the cradle to the grave.

Let us first briefly review the situation Jesus confronted. During his lifetime his people were subject to Rome. Palestine was a minor Roman province. His contemporaries chafed under Roman rule. Once they had been a theocracy —God alone was their king and ruler. It was not until the days of Samuel that they requested a king, and Samuel, as you recall, anointed Saul to be the first king of Israel. Under David and Solomon the kingdom had flourished, but now for some three centuries Israel had struggled with Greeks, Syrians, and Romans to achieve their freedom. This proud people were ruled by foreigners. Resentment ran high, so much so that during the Passover, when thousands of pilgrims came from far and wide to Jerusalem, Rome took particular precautions against possible uprisings.

Such uprisings, aimed at throwing off the Roman yoke, occurred frequently—the book of Acts records two of them, one headed by Theudas and the other by Judas of Galilee. These would-be deliverers, unsuccessful though they were, were symbolic of the Deliverer, the Messiah, who some day would come to free Israel from her subservience to Rome. Jesus' contemporaries were "waiting for the consolation of Israel." Luke gives us three of the earliest hymns of the church: the Magnificat of Mary, the Benedictus of Zacharias, and the Nunc Dimittis of Simeon. You cannot read these beautiful poems without sensing the martial spirit that pervades them. They are indeed strange cradle songs. Mary in her Magnificat sings of God who "hath shewed strength with his arm, . . . hath put down the mighty from their seats, and exalted them of low degree." Zacharias speaks of being "saved from our enemies, and from the hand of all that hate us, . . . that we being delivered out of the hand of our enemies might serve him without fear." And the aged Simeon speaks of "the glory of thy people Israel."

There were different ideas as to the kind of deliverer who would carry out this program of Israel's liberation. Broadly speaking, all these ideas could be summarized under two heads. For some the promised deliverer was conceived as a warrior king who would lead an insurrection against Rome and so lift by military force the Roman yoke. For others the deliverer was a heavenly being who with legions of angels and flaming swords would destroy the pagan world and establish a messianic empire. In either event, however, whether the deliverer was regarded as an earthly king heading an army or a celestial being surrounded by the heavenly hosts, the objective was the same: the restoration of the kingdom of Israel, a kingdom modeled after the Davidic dynasty, with its capital in Jerusalem and possessed of the particularisms of race and nation—essentially a nationalistic kingdom.

That kingdom is well described by Daniel: "And in the days of these kings shall the God of heaven set up a kingdom, which shall never be destroyed: and the kingdom shall not be left to other people, but it shall break in pieces and consume all these kingdoms, and it shall stand for ever." [1] Even when such militaristic or nationalistic conceptions are softened and spiritualized, still the favored position of Israel is taken for granted. The messianic kingdom would be patterned after the nationalistic Davidic dynasty.

It is my contention that Jesus fulfilled neither of these messianic expectations, that he regarded himself not as the son of David but rather as the Son of man. Many instances in the Gospels indicate as much. In his parable of the good Samaritan he speaks of "a certain man [who] went down from Jerusalem to Jericho." The man's race, nationality, creed, social position, are all irrelevant. The important thing is that he was a man. Jesus denounces Jewish leaders and praises Roman centurions. He describes the kingdom as one to which "many shall come from the east and west,

[1] Dan. 2:44.

and shall sit down with Abraham, and Isaac, and Jacob," while "the children of the kingdom shall be cast out into outer darkness." In the judgment scene he says that before God "shall be gathered all nations." He tells his disciples to go "into all the world, and preach the gospel to every creature." He once said: "Whosoever shall do the will of my Father which is in heaven, the same is my brother, and sister, and mother."

Without going into much further detail we might consider what is perhaps the most striking instance of his departure from the traditional messianic conception, with its nationalistic emphasis, the Palm Sunday episode. Jesus is surrounded by adoring multitudes whose enthusiastic behavior evidences the fact that they think their hopes are being fulfilled. He knows, however, that their hosannas are based on a misconception. "Blessed be the King that cometh in the name of the Lord," they cry. They were right in their phraseology but wrong in the content they gave it. They called him a king. He was. But he was not the kind of king they thought he was, and the kind that he was they did not want. They thought he was going to a throne; he knew he was going to a cross. They thought he was going to redeem Israel; he knew his mission was to redeem the world. They expected him to set up a kingdom which would give pre-eminence and power to their country; he envisioned the establishment of the frontierless kingdom of God. When they discovered the true nature of his kingdom and kingship their jubilant cries were silenced; nay, rather they changed them from "hosanna" to "crucify"!

Ostensibly then Jesus was condemned to death by Pilate because he was a dangerous rival of Caesar. Actually his contemporaries had him crucified because he was not dangerous. The kingdom he proclaimed and the kingship he revealed were alike foreign to the popular mind. Even his own disciples did not fully understand. In the beautiful Emmaus story they said of him: "We trusted that it had been he which should have redeemed Israel."

The decision of the Master to move out beyond the traditional nationalistic hopes and expectations of his people into ampler areas of thought and action was made during what was in some ways the most crucial experience of his life, the temptation. However we interpret it, this event marks the turning point in Jesus' ministry. Here in the wilderness he repudiated all that was connected with the traditional "son of David" concept. He was shown the kingdoms of the world and all the glory of them. He turned his back upon this glory for a greater glory—the glory of God. The nature of this glory he was soon to reveal in the Sermon on the Mount, which may be regarded as the blueprint of the kingdom he came to establish. The beatitudes of his spiritual, and therefore universal, kingdom stand in sharp contrast to those of the nationalistic kingdoms of this world. Blessed are the strong, for they shall conquer the earth—so it is in the kingdoms of the world. But in his kingdom: "Blessed are the meek: for they shall inherit the earth." Blessed are they that persecute for revenge or sadism; but in his kingdom: "Blessed are they which are persecuted for righteousness' sake." Blessed are they that hunger and thirst after power and prestige; but in his kingdom: "Blessed are they which do hunger and thirst after righteousness." Blessed are the warmongers, for thus they think to conquer the world. "Blessed are the peacemakers: for they shall be called the children of God."

It seems to me that it is impossible to reconcile the ideals of the Sermon on the Mount with the traditional nationalistic concept of the kingdom. Jesus' contemporaries were seeking a warrior king, but he was the kind of king who would conquer by love and establish his kingdom, not in Jerusalem, but in men's hearts. Robert Bridges, late poet laureate of England, has expressed this truth beautifully:

> So it was when Jesus came in his gentleness
> with his divine compassion and great Gospel of Peace,
> men hail'd him WORD OF GOD, and in the title of Christ
> crown'd him with love beyond all earth-names of renown.
> For He, wandering unarm'd save by the Spirit's flame,
> in few years with few friends founded a world-empire
> wider than Alexander's and more enduring;
> since from his death it took its everlasting life.
> HIS kingdom is God's kingdom, and his holy temple
> not in Athens or Rome but in the heart of man.[2]

The evils of nationalism are so well known that I need not rehearse them here. I should rather like to point out the basic and unalterable incongruity, if not positive opposition, of the message of Jesus to this appalling curse which now threatens the destruction of mankind. This I shall do by considering what Jesus meant by the phrase "the kingdom of God."

It is indeed an ambitious undertaking for any but a New Testament scholar—a position to which I lay no claim whatever—to say what the Master may have meant by this

---

[2] *The Testament of Beauty* (Oxford: Clarendon Press, 1929) , p. 40.

phrase. All of us would agree, however, whether we be
scholars or not, that the phrase "the kingdom of God" is
the heart of Jesus' message. We read that after John was
put in prison, "Jesus went about all Galilee . . . preaching
the gospel of the kingdom." Many questions arise as we
contemplate the "kingdom." Will the kingdom ever come
in this world or must it await some other for its consum-
mation? Will the kingdom come gradually, like the breaking of the dawn, or suddenly, as light comes into a darkened
room? Is it to be brought by God alone, by man alone, or
by God and man working co-operatively? Is it a reality
which is wholly in the future, or might it in some sense be
regarded as being present already? Is the church a means
to the bringing of the kingdom, or is it an earnest or fore-
taste of the kingdom—"the little flock" to whom God will
"give" the kingdom? What must one do to enter the kingdom? Who are qualified to be citizens thereof?

These are all important and legitimate questions. But
let us venture now to face an even more basic one, namely,
What did Jesus mean when he used the phrase "the kingdom of God"? Was it to him a "supernatural," "super-
historical" reality, a "tremendous eschatological drama"?
Or did Jesus by his use of the phrase think of the kingdom
as being socially and ethically relevant to his age? These
questions open up a highly technical and speculative field
of inquiry. Albert Schweitzer's answer would be that
Jesus' view of the kingdom was wholly otherworldly, eschatological, apocalyptic. At the other extreme would be the
answer of the rabid social-gospeler, who would claim that
could we but establish socialism we should no longer need
the church, since we should have established the kingdom

71

of God on earth! Between these extremes would be the view of those scholars who agree that eschatology was present in the thinking of Jesus, providing the background of his thought, but that it was not prominent nor decisive in his thinking. It seems difficult to understand Jesus' numerous parables of the kingdom without the supposition that he regarded it as being in some sense ethically relevant to his age and so to ours. "If I cast out devils by the Spirit of God, then the kingdom of God is come unto you." [3] Perhaps Charles H. Dodd comes near the truth by his use of the phrase "realized eschatology." He writes in *The Parables of the Kingdom*: "It appears that while Jesus employed the . . . symbolism of apocalypse to indicate the 'other-worldly' or absolute character of the Kingdom of God, He used parables to enforce and illustrate the idea that the Kingdom of God had come upon men there and then."

While scholars debate, however, ordinary people like you and me should come to some conclusion as to what this phrase means to them. Every Sunday the minister leads his congregation in the Lord's Prayer—"Thy kingdom come, thy will be done in earth, as it is in heaven." Well now, suppose that prayer were answered, suppose the kingdom should come, should we recognize it if we saw it? It seems to me that if we are to pray intelligently, "Thy kingdom come," we should have some idea of what we are praying for. What, after all, would our society be like if God's will were done on earth as it is in heaven?

The key to the answer is furnished, as I think, in Jesus' statement to Pilate: "My kingdom is not of this world."

[3] Matt. 12:28.

72

Did he mean to say that the kingdom could never fully come in this world, or that its ideals were incompatible with the standards of this world?—or both? Whatever he may have meant, let us proceed *in the light of the Cross* to discover some of the ways in which Jesus' kingdom differs from the nationalistic kingdoms of the world and so conflicts with them.

For one thing, it appears that his kingdom differs from the kingdoms of this world in its very nature. The kingdoms of this world are material, physical entities, but surely when we pray "Thy kingdom come" we envisage no such reality. When we pray "Thy kingdom come" we are not thinking, are we, of some political state with an earthly ruler, geographical boundaries, and foreign diplomats, with appropriations for armies and navies, and taxation and passports, and all that sort of thing? We are rather thinking of a spiritual state or condition that results from the rule of God, the rule of righteousness and love in the hearts of men. The kingdom of God is a moral and spiritual reality, not a material entity. "The fruit of the Spirit is love, joy, peace, longsuffering, gentleness, goodness, faith . . . ," wrote Paul to the Galatians. "The kingdom of God is within you," said Jesus. This does not mean that the kingdom is subjective or private. There is another translation—"The kingdom of God is among you." Both are right. Indeed, the proof of its inner reality or vitality is in its outer manifestations. The inner spiritual reality of the kingdom is seen in that it insinuates itself into all the relationships of life. Like the leaven, its presence must be felt throughout the whole lump.

It follows, in the second place, that the scale of values of Jesus' kingdom is different from that of the nationalistic kingdoms of this world. It uses a different yardstick, so to speak. In the kingdoms of this world the measurements are quantitative. Somehow we feel instinctively that in the kingdom of God such measurements are not primary. For the kingdom of God, as we have seen, is a spiritual kingdom. It is qualitative, and we cannot apply quantitative measurements to qualitative values. It is evident that Jesus expected the kingdom and those who are citizens of it to be different from the world. "Ye are the light of the world" —not the world. And "the salt of the earth"—not the earth. And the "leaven" in the lump—not the lump. So different was the kingdom to be that to enter it one had to lay aside all his inherited ideas of pomp and power and greatness, and become as a little child. So different that in this kingdom the greatest would be the servant. Those who by worldly standards were first would be the last. From the point of view of the kingdom of God, the greatest church is not necessarily the church with the largest membership or the biggest budget or the most varied and numerous organizations and activities. The church that met in Jerusalem at the time of Pentecost was by quantitative standards insignificant. But from the point of view of its creative life it was one of the greatest churches of all time. "Silver and gold have I none," said Peter, its leading spirit; "but such as I have give I." From the point of view of the kingdom the question is not how many but what sort.

You may recall the story of the old preacher who said that he had had a great revival in his church. Somebody asked him how many had been added to the membership, and he replied, "We did not add any, but we dropped a hundred." Every church naturally wants to grow numerically—a surplus is always more impressive than a deficit—and yet we must keep reminding ourselves that from the point of view of the kingdom of God, quantitative tests are not first nor final. As far as the church is concerned the question, I repeat, is not how many but what sort. What are the citizens of the kingdom thinking, what opinions do they hold, what are their ideals? How much vision do they have? Is there that about them which makes them different from the rank and file? Are they dough or leaven? The qualitative test is the Christian test. Maybe the church will have to be smaller before it becomes bigger.

"My kingdom is not of this world" because, in the third place, it has no boundaries. It is a frontierless kingdom, unmarked by all the particularisms of race and nationality. It is here that Jesus' concept of the kingdom comes into head-on collision with the nationalistic kingdoms of this world. This is the proof that his kingdom is the kingdom of truth. Truth is universal. Whatever is really true anywhere is true everywhere. Truth, too, is absolute, and whatever is genuinely true any time is true for all time. The kingdom, then, because it is a kingdom of truth, proclaimed by one who said, "I am . . . the truth," is universal. Whenever we pray "Thy kingdom come" we are praying not for any one nation but for all mankind. The kingdom of God is not national. It is universal, world wide.

On this point of the universality of the kingdom one encounters considerable disagreement. There is certainly another point of view. The following is a typical way of putting it: "In no word of his [Jesus] do we find him transcending Israel and speaking to Man in general. Jesus was a Jew—in blood, in loyalty, in mental outlook, in his criticism of Jewry, in his positive message." [4] There are two statements of Jesus which are usually quoted in support of such a position. In Matthew it is written about the sending out of the twelve: "These twelve Jesus sent forth, and commanded them, saying, Go not into the way of the Gentiles, and into any city of the Samaritans enter ye not: but go rather to the lost sheep of the house of Israel." The other statement, from the same book, is in reference to the healing of the daughter of the Syrophoenician woman. In answer to her appeal that her daughter be healed, Jesus is said to have replied: "I am not sent but unto the lost sheep of the house of Israel. Then came she and worshipped him, saying, Lord, help me. But he answered and said, It is not meet to take the children's bread, and to cast it to dogs." To which she replied: "Truth, Lord: yet the dogs eat of the crumbs which fall from their masters' table." Bernard Shaw once commented that by this statement the Syrophoenician woman made Jesus a Christian—a very clever but in my judgment a wholly false assertion.

Actually, if there be any two statements in the New Testament the authenticity of which I should question in that they do not seem like the Master, these are they! I regard them as expressive of the spirit of Matthew—who has given us the most Jewish Gospel—rather than of the spirit of Christ. But suppose Jesus did make them—what of it? To select these two statements as representative of the Man who meets us in the Gospels is, it seems to me, to yield to a strange mental bias. Sometimes a wind blow-

[4] *The Christian Century*, Dec. 20, 1939, p. 1567.

ing offshore meets an incoming tide and starts surface ripples moving in the opposite direction. The ripples on the
surface are moving seaward, but the tide which runs deeper
and stronger is moving in. It is hard to read the Gospels
and escape the conclusion that the underlying current of
Jesus' life and message was away from the particularisms of
his race and nation and toward universalism. As the well-
known Scottish scholar James Mackinnon said in *The Gospel in the Early Church:* "One who emphasized the Fatherhood of God and sought to spiritualize the current
Judaism could hardly have conceived of his Messianic vo-
cation in the exclusive, as he certainly did not in the nationalist sense."

To say, as do some, that the universalist note in the
Gospels did not originate with Jesus but was attributed to
him later by the Gentile church, when it became univer-
salistic, is not convincing. No more are we convinced by
the argument so often made that Paul, not Jesus, was the
man who made Christianity universal by taking it to the
Gentiles. If we had never seen one of the epistles of Paul
and had been compelled to confine our knowledge of
Jesus and his message purely to the Gospels, I for one do
not believe we could be true to those Gospels and keep
Christianity within our race or nation. Every essential
teaching or emphasis of Paul, as John Baillie of Edinburgh
pointed out long ago, is rooted in the mind of Jesus of
Nazareth, especially, I should add, this emphasis on universalism. Paul was "an Hebrew of the Hebrews; as touching
the law, a Pharisee." But Christ made shipwreck of this
exclusiveness. "He . . . hath broken down the middle wall
of partition between us," said Paul. In him "there is neither

Greek nor Jew, circumcision nor uncircumcision, Barbarian, Scythian, bond nor free." Kenneth Scott Latourette, in *The Unquenchable Light,* writes: "The contrast between Judaism and Christianity was partly between the universality of Christianity, its appeal to all men regardless of race or culture, and the persistent and narrow tribalism of Judaism. This, as Stephen and Paul saw, went back to Jesus himself." Adolf von Harnack speaks of the "implicit universalism" of the gospel. Ernest Findlay Scott speaks of the gospel as being "inherently universal."

Along with the universal nature of the gospel goes its spiritual hospitality, its grace and graciousness. God makes his sun to shine on the evil and the good. He leaves the ninety and nine to seek the one that is lost. He bids us go beyond duty to love, which never says, "I have done enough," but asks, "What more may I do?" "What do ye more than others?" asked Christ. The righteousness of God in orthodox Jewry was thought of largely in terms of justice and merit. To Jesus, God's righteousness manifested itself in terms of unmerited grace. The universality of the kingdom then was evident not only geographically but also in its spiritual concern for all sorts and conditions of men: not only the good but the bad, not only the whole but the sick, not only the saved but the lost. It is the kingdom of One the length and breadth of whose love passes our knowledge.

It follows, in the fourth place, that the kingdom is not of this world in that it cannot be established by the methods of this world. "My kingdom is not of this world: if my kingdom were of this world, then would my servants fight," Jesus said to Pilate. You will recall, too, that when the mob came to arrest Jesus, Peter drew a sword, and Jesus said to him: "Put up again thy sword into his place: for all they that take the sword shall perish with the sword." It is forever true that in the kingdom of God, because it is spiritual, the opposition is spiritual: "For we wrestle not against flesh and blood, but . . . against the rulers of the darkness of this world, against spiritual wickedness in high places." [5]

To say this is not to say that force has no bearing on or no place in the plan of God, yet its place is never a final nor decisive one. Take the second World War, for example. Does anyone think that the victory the allied armies have won is of itself an assurance or guarantee of a better, saner, and happier world, a world nearer the pattern of the kingdom? Nothing could be farther from the truth. Were not our arms victorious twenty-five years ago? Where is the better world? All that force can do is to crush or restrain the aggressive forces of evil and so give us a chance to build a better world. But that better world must be built with other weapons than the weapons of the flesh. "Be not overcome of evil, but overcome evil with good." So Jesus set out to win men, not conquer them— or rather to conquer them not with the weapons of the flesh but of the spirit, by love: "And I, if I be lifted up, . . . will draw all men unto me." "Ye know that the princes of the Gentiles exercise dominion over them, and they that are great exercise authority upon them. But it shall not be so among you." His method was love and persuasion, means compatible with the spiritual ends he envisioned.

Here then were four marks of the kingdom of God

[5] Eph. 6:12.

as Jesus proclaimed it. It was spiritual, not material; qualitative, not quantitative; universal, not local; expressive of creative love, not force. This concept his people did not fully understand. Even on his way to the cross an ambitious mother was requesting that her sons be given the chief seats in the kingdom, forgetting that the greatest in his kingdom is the servant of all. The spiritual marks of his kingdom were not compatible with the kingdom of Israel, a nationalistic kingdom with Jerusalem as its center, and one race holding a favored position. There was therefore a severe conflict between Jesus and his generation. The man in whom the disappointment of his contemporaries found expression was in my judgment Judas Iscariot.

We have not always understood this strange man of Kerioth. Why did Judas betray Jesus? Consider some of the motives attributed to him. Avarice is one: "thirty pieces of silver." The mercenary motive may have entered in, but we may be certain it was not the primary one. Had it been, would he not have played for higher stakes?

Jealousy is another explanation. This is more plausible. Judas was the only Judean among the disciples. All the others were from Galilee, and Galileans were not held in very high regard by Judeans. By its location to the north Galilee was subject to a constant infiltration by Greeks and Romans. This mingling of the nations was an offense to the Jews, who regarded the Galileans as a people of mixed blood. Judea, to the south, on the other hand had been the home of the greatest of Israel. The proudest memories of Israel's past were associated with its name. Judas was from Judea, yet, strangely enough, these Galileans, supposedly inferior folk, had come to leadership among the disciples. Peter, James, and John, Galileans all, had shared with Jesus certain experiences from which Judas had been excluded. This hurt his pride, made him jealous. If Jesus had no need for him, he knew that Caiaphas had, and he would show these Galileans how important this Judean really was. There is no doubt truth in this interpretation. Nor would it be the first time that a man betrayed a movement because he felt he did not occupy as prominent a position of leadership in it as he thought he deserved.

There was no doubt then jealousy and avarice in Judas—but neither one in my judgment explains his act. It is true that were we to confine ourselves to the direct evidence of the Gospels we could reach no other conclusion. There is, however, indirect evidence for the position, usually attributed to Thomas De Quincey and now shared by many, that Judas was a disillusioned nationalist.[6] I share the view of those New Testament scholars and writers who believe that Judas betrayed Jesus because he was a disillusioned and disappointed man.[7] The kingdom as he envisioned it was the Davidic kingdom restored in all its glory, with Israel possessor of the power and prestige. It was a nationalistic kingdom. Jesus on the contrary visualized a universal kingdom. But this concept Judas could not understand.

One can imagine this proud Judean, in whose heart glowed the hope of Israel's restoration, saying to himself

[6] See *Judas Iscariot,* Vol. VIII of *The Collected Writings of Thomas De Quincey,* ed. David Masson (A. C. Black, 1896-97) , pp. 177 ff.
[7] See Walter Russell Bowie, *The Master:A Life of Jesus Christ,* pp. 262 f.

during the last week of Jesus' earthly life: "Why did he on his triumphant entry refuse the proffered crown? What does he mean by 'Blessed are the meek'? Whoever heard of a meek king? What can he mean when he speaks of Messiah going to Jerusalm to suffer and die? What a fine climax this is for the long-looked-for deliverer of our nation! What does he mean when he says, 'Love your enemies," when those enemies have invaded your capital city? 'Pray for them that despitefully use you,' when such people stalk your streets? Maybe I do not understand him. I must find out. And the way for me to find out is to put him in a position where he will have to act. I will arrange it so that this man who claims to represent and possess the power of God will be brought face to face with earthly power. Maybe then he will summon his legions of angels to deliver him." His betrayal was an attempt to force Jesus' hand. His mind was torn between "disappointment and tempestuous hope." Even if his motives may not have been quite so sinister as we have supposed, still I believe with Henry Sloane Coffin that in forcing Jesus to declare himself, he "did it vindictively, not affectionately." Sholem Asch in *The Nazarene* has Jesus say to Judas: "Judah, thy heart is restless, it is like a lost ship in a stormy sea. Why canst thou not find rest, like my other disciples?" And Judas replies: "Rabbi, perform now one of thy wonders and strengthen my faith in thee." But he performed no wonder. Peter drew his sword—the weapon Israel's deliverer was expected to use—and Jesus said: "Put up . . . thy sword; . . . they that take the sword shall perish with the sword." As if to say, "This kingdom of mine uses other weapons."

For not with swords loud clashing,
Nor roll of stirring drums;
With deeds of love and mercy,
The heavenly kingdom comes.

Nationalism then crucified Jesus. His message of the kingdom of God was directly opposed to it. He was not the warrior king in line with the Davidic tradition, whose task it was to throw off the Roman yoke and restore the kingdom of Israel. This was the leader they wanted. But he could not give them what they wanted, and they did not want what he had to give and so they crucified him.

Nationalism is still one of Christianity's most formidable rivals. It is, as far as the general welfare of mankind is concerned, perhaps our greatest single menace. In our time we have seen the spirit of nationalism at a high-water mark in the fanatical totalitarian regimes in which man becomes a puppet, the helpless, subservient tool of the all-powerful state, his body, mind and soul cowed and subdued, since in totalitarianism a man cannot even call his soul his own. The thoroughgoing conflict between the totalitarian regimes and the Christian gospel was clearly seen even by those who thought the regimes should not have been opposed by force. Not so many people, however, see so clearly the problem which nationalism in its less extreme form still presents, now that totalitarianism has been largely conquered and the liberty of the individual guaranteed in theory at least.

For while nationalism as we now practice it does not enslave or oppress the individual, it threatens the life of the race. It may soberly be said that the only hope for mankind today lies in supplanting his now utterly suicidal competitive nationalistic policies with co-operative international ones. Bertrand Russell may have spoken truly when he said that only in giving up national sovereignty can man survive, but that man will not give up sovereignty because ninety per cent of the human race would rather be dead than sensible. The greatest obstacle in the way of man's survival is the fetish of national sovereignties, which Norman Cousins justly calls "vestigial obstructions in the circulatory system of the world."

The crux of the conflict between nationalism and Christianity lies in this, that whereas nationalism puts first the welfare of the nation, Christianity puts first the welfare of mankind: "For God so loved the world . . ." The so-called realist may be wont to regard this emphasis of Jesus upon the welfare of all men, regardless of race, class, or nation, as being a wild bit of sentimentalism. In the providence of God, however, it is now evident to all but the hopelessly blind that in this teaching of Jesus lies the only way out. For the welfare of the nation now, of any nation, is utterly dependent on the welfare of all nations. The day is gone forever when any nation, be it one of the so-called "Big Three"—a designation which I have come thoroughly to dislike—or a little nation, can be permanently prosperous or secure if it indulges in policies of injustice or oppression.

Unfortunately, the powers that be, even with two world wars staring them in the face, do not yet seem fully to understand this. "The god of this world hath blinded the minds of them which believe not." In so far as the victorious

84

nations, acting together or acting singly, indulge in tragically shortsighted policies of vengeance, injustice, greed, or oppression, they are only burying time bombs which some day will explode and involve the entire human race in war. We can only hope and pray that the powers that be will become aware of the realities of the situation before it is too late.

This emphasis of Jesus on the world rather than any particular nation, on humanity rather than a particular race or class, is vindicated today. To be sure, he was not the first to think in terms of world community. Before his birth there were occasional flashes of light, fitful and intermittent, that illumined the darkness. Thinkers of ancient times, such as Confucius, Heraclitus, Plato, Terence, had caught glimpses of the truth of world community. But with the coming of Christ the dawn broke, the sun rose high in the heavens. In Christ these occasional and intermittent flashes became a clear and steady glow, radiant as the noonday sun. With Christ came One who was to be the light of the world. It is impossible to set Jesus and his message within the framework of any one race, class, or nation.

To build a world consciousness, a world community, is the task before our generation. No task is more important. Can we do it in time to stave off calamity? The task will not be easy. As proof, witness our own country. At the conclusion of the American Civil War in 1865, the Triennial Convention of the Protestant Episcopal Church proposed a new form of prayer which began with the petition, "O God, the only Lord and Ruler of all the peoples upon earth, bless this our nation." But the form of the prayer was rejected. The feeling between the North and South was too strong. So instead of saying, "Bless this our nation," they said, "Bless these United States." [8] And this, mark you, among peoples who had a common language, a common government, and, we might almost say, a common race, since in 1865 the British element was dominant. And yet we did not have one nation. That shows you how hard it will be to have one world. The encouraging part of the problem, however, is that whereas two thousand years ago Jesus was by and large the lone voice crying in the wilderness, today many voices are saying "One world."

Big business says "One world." It knows no frontiers. But big business will not give us one world, for it is competitive, not cohesive.

Government is saying "One world." Some fifty-two nations have just formed the United Nations. Essential, however, as is that organization, it cannot give us one world. Perhaps next to Woodrow Wilson, Lord Robert Cecil had more to do with the League of Nations than any other one man. When the Covenant was finally finished, his brother Hugh said to him, "Lord Robert, will the League work?" And Lord Robert replied, "Think again, Hugh. Does a spade work?" The United Nations Organization is only an instrument. It is no panacea. It will not work of itself. The key to its success lies not in it but in us.

Science is saying "One world." It has made the world a geographic unit. Nothing is remote any more. The "Globester" circles our little planet now in less than 150 hours. The radio sends our voice around the world in a

---

[8] From Leyton Richards, *Realistic Pacificism,* p. 139.

fraction of a second. But science has not and cannot give us one world. All it has done is to make it impossible for us to avoid each other. Physical proximity does not mean unity; it may mean destruction. Science seems to be saying to us, "I have brought you all together and there is no backing away—either unite or perish." Actually science has played a rather mean trick on us. Just now that it has brought us within easy reach of each other, it has given us the atomic bomb! Now that it has literally put our fences together it has given us a weapon of incredible destructiveness, which, by the use of rocket planes, we can hurl at each other as easily as throwing a brick over the back fence. Proximity plus power means peril, and it is that peril we now confront.

Here then is the situation: Business, government, and science have, after two thousand years, begun to appreciate somewhat Jesus' concept of human solidarity. They are all saying now what he said long ago: "One world." But though they say "One world" they cannot create one world, for real unity is spiritual. That is why Christ and his gospel of the kingdom is still the hope of the world. For Christianity, too, says "One world." Ah, yes, but Christianity has the power to make the world one. Because, unlike business, government, or science, its first aim is to create and impart spiritual unity. Its message is that we are all children of one Father and so brothers one of another. This was the good news Christ commissioned his disciples to preach to all the world: "Tell every creature that he is a child of God and so a brother of his fellow man." This is the gospel of salvation for the world. For it is the soil in which good will and therefore peace is rooted.

For two thousand years that gospel has been proclaimed. Every country, though not every creature, has heard it; but no country has fully believed it. Now the best informed among us are saying: "You had better believe it, and live it. If you do not, the alternative may be destruction."

See how this sense of spiritual unity really unites and transcends nationalism. An African Christian addressing an American audience once said, "I don't want to be called an African Christian. I am a Christian from Africa." In 1942 the Christians of Japan refused to call their church "The United Church of Japan." They chose the name, "The United Church *in* Japan." A boy in northern India was about to take his examinations. He was in a Christian school. He prayed for God's help and this was his prayer: "Our Father, help me to pass my examinations. May my whole class pass. May the whole school pass. May the whole world pass." [9] So whether in Africa, Japan, or India, genuine Christianity produces this world consciousness. That boy's prayer must be ours.

It is evident that we must begin to think now in world terms. We must, by the grace of God, outgrow our insularity, pettiness, and provincialism. If we do not they may become our epitaph. For from now on we are going to have one world—or none!

[9] From *The World at One in Prayer*, ed. Daniel J. Fleming, p. 74.

IV

Opportunism: *Pilate*

PILATE is one of the prominent characters of Holy Week. His role in the crucifixion of Jesus is a decisive one: he could either release or sentence him. He sentenced him to death. His part in the crucifixion has given rise to interesting and strange stories. One is that he committed suicide. Another, that he was beheaded. A third, that his body, weighted with lead, was thrown into the Tiber, yet despite this, would not sink. A fourth, that his body was thrown into a small lake in Switzerland near Mount Pilatos, and that every year on the anniversary of the trial the body reappears on the surface and washes its guilty hands in vain regret.

I rather think, however, that Anatole France, in his justly famous story "The Procurator of Judea," has given us a truer picture. He describes Pilate, who had retired to Sicily, taking a cure at a summer resort. Here he meets an old friend, Laelius Lamia by name. They reminisce about Judea, its times and its peoples. Finally Lamia mentions the fact of the crucifixion of Jesus and asks: "Pontius, do you remember anything about the man?" Pilate is silent, as though trying to recall some distant memory. "Jesus? Jesus—of Nazareth?" he answers. "I cannot call him to mind." Yet today we are calling Pilate to mind solely because of his connection with Jesus. But for that, this petty Roman governor who ruled over one of the smallest of the Roman provinces, Judea, would long since have been forgotten. So time alters the opinions of men, and in the perspective of history many judgments are reversed—none more so than the one handed down in Pilate's judgment hall of the long ago.

Opinions differ as to how much blame should be attached to the Roman procurator for the crucifixion. Some say he is entirely to blame. This is the position of Joseph Klausner. He maintains that, although the Scriptures blame the Jews for the crucifixion, the real culprit is Pilate. He says that the Scriptures present Pilate in a favorable light because the early Christians needed his support and protection, which they could not have obtained had they laid the blame on him. Therefore they made a scapegoat of the Pharisees and Sadducees. Precisely the opposite point of view is propounded by James Black of Edinburgh. After reading his defense of Pilate in his book *Rogues of the Bible,* one is tempted to say that were he not so eminently effective a clergyman he had spoiled a good barrister. His argument is very simple. As a judge Pilate was obligated to administer Roman law. Jesus was accused of being a political insurrectionist. "Pilate asked him, 'Are you the king of the Jews?' He replied, 'Certainly.' " [1] That is to say, Jesus pleaded guilty to the charge. Under the circumstances, Pilate had no choice but to sentence him. Dr. Black's position, therefore, is that it was not Pilate who crucified Jesus but Roman law treacherously used by the priests for their own end. It might help us to make up our own minds if we briefly review the trial.

The charge brought against Jesus was: "We found this

[1] Luke 23:3—Moffatt.

fellow perverting the nation, and forbidding to give tribute to Caesar, saying that he himself is Christ a King." No more serious charge could have been brought against a Jew in Jesus' day than that of political ambition. Caesar was exceedingly jealous for his throne and had decreed that anyone in his sane mind who claimed kingship was guilty of treason, the punishment for which was invariably death. On the face of it then, it appears as though Pilate in sentencing Jesus to death was only doing his duty. It is my judgment, however, that we cannot decide this matter "on the face of it"—it is not so simple as that. For though Jesus pleaded guilty to the charge of being a king, Pilate knew very well that the kingship of which Jesus spoke was not the kind that Caesar needed to fear, since it was not in the slightest sense political.

The proof that it was not was evident, strangely enough, from the very fact that Jesus stood accused by his compatriots of being a political revolutionary. They were looking for a warrior king who would lead an insurrection against Rome. Had Jesus been such a one, it is hardly conceivable that they would have brought him before Pilate. On the contrary, they would have regarded him as a national hero and given him their wholehearted support. So that it was precisely because Jesus was not politically dangerous, but advocated giving tribute to Caesar, that he was brought before Pilate. Pilate certainly knew that, and such knowledge was in itself proof conclusive that Jesus was innocent of the crime of which he stood accused. If, however, further proof were needed, it could be found in the expedients to which Pilate resorted in his re-

peated attempts not to condemn an innocent man. Let
us briefly review these expedients.

One of them was in sending him to Herod. Herod, who
was in Jerusalem for the Passover, was Tetrarch of Galilee. Pilate saw in this coincidence a handy way of getting
a disagreeable job off his hands. So he sent Jesus to Herod,
since Jesus was from Galilee. But Herod apparently was
not in a judicial mood, and sent Jesus back to Pilate. Pilate
then suggested that Jesus be scourged instead of crucified.
He himself was not permitted to substitute scourging for
crucifixion, but by the suggestion he was making it possible
for the Jews to change their charge from treason to some
less dangerous one. "I will therefore chastise him, and release him." But this expedient also failed. Then he tried
another. There was a custom that at the time of the Passover some prisoner should be released. There was a noto-
rious criminal and rebel—one Barabbas—charged with rob-
bery and murder. Pilate would have the public choose
between him and Jesus. The mob decided in favor of
Barabbas, and so that expedient failed also.

But Pilate did not yet give up hope. There were two
other devices he could try. One was the gesture of washing
his hands. Traditionally the Jews were afraid of having innocent blood on their heads. It was Pilate's hope that by
this gesture their ancient superstitious fear might overcome their determined intent. But this, too, failed. The
gesture did not divert them from their avowed purpose.
His last device is disclosed in his statement: "Behold the
man!" This was an attempt to win by sympathy or even
pity what he had failed to win by persuasion or by reason-
ing. Scourging was a part of the drama of crucifixion. It

was not a gratuitous cruelty. So by bringing forth the Christ after he had been scourged and pointing to his pathetic figure, Pilate no doubt hoped to soften the heart of the mob. "Behold the man." "Surely," Pilate must have thought, "that will melt their hearts." But it did not.

Now certainly no judge who believes a prisoner guilty would go to such lengths to procure his acquittal. The fact that Pilate resorted to these expedients would seem to prove that he was certain of Jesus' innocence. He said so: "For he knew that for envy they had delivered him." What if Jesus did assert that he was a king? Pilate knew that the kingship and the kingdom he proclaimed had nothing in common with the kingship or the kingdom whose rivalry Tiberius feared. Yet he sentenced him to die. Why? The answer to that question reveals one of the great sources of injustice and evil in the world from that time even until now, namely, opportunism.

Who is an opportunist? He is a politician in the current connotation of that word. Not all such politicians are in government service. Some may be found in business, some in the professions, and I should not be too surprised if one or two may be found even in the church! The opportunist is one who acts from policy rather than principle, from expediency rather than conviction. He does not steer his course by any fixed point but by the way the wind is blowing. He has no deep convictions and so, like the double-minded man, unstable in all his ways, is driven with the wind and tossed. He looks around him and keeps his ear to the ground. "If thou let this man go, thou art not Caesar's friend." "And so Pilate, willing to content the

people, . . . delivered Jesus . . . to be crucified." Willing
to content the people!

Who are we to condemn this politician for playing safe?
He knew from experience that a course displeasing to
the Jews would not further his own political interests.
Two of his previous experiences with them taught him
that. Once he had ordered his legions to march into Jerusalem carrying standards bearing the Emperor's effigy.
The Jews resented this because it was too much like emperor worship. Previous governors had respected their
wishes; Pilate would not. The Jews requested that the
standards be removed; Pilate refused, but so adamant and
relentless was their opposition that finally he was forced
to back down. On another occasion Pilate had some shields
engraved with the Emperor's name and hung them in the
palace at Jerusalem. Again the populace was disturbed and
appealed to Pilate. Again he refused. But the priests did
not accept his refusal. They sent a delegation to Rome,
secretly, and laid their grievance before the Emperor, who
wrote a letter to Pilate rebuking him and commanding
him to remove the shields, which he did. From these two
incidents the priests had learned two lessons: "first, that
persistency could break mere obstinacy; and second, that
veiled threats of appeal to Rome might work the oracle." [2]

Now once again Pilate faced his subjects. Their twice-
won victory over him was not reassuring as he heard their
insistent demands. His position was a difficult one. The
problem he faced was not that of deciding whether Jesus
was guilty or innocent. He knew he was innocent; he
said so. The problem was whether he should acquit an

[2] James Black, *op. cit.*

94

innocent man and so infuriate the populace, who might very well have sent another secret embassy to Caesar, or sentence an innocent man to death and so establish himself more securely in the affections of his subjects. Pilate's problem was not one of law, it was a problem of conscience; and as Shakespeare once put it, "thus conscience does make cowards of us all." Here was a man who knew what the right course was and deep in his heart may have wanted to follow it. He did not want to condemn Jesus to death. But to acquit him was to endanger his own position. Pilate had political ambitions; he was anxious to win and hold imperial favor. He must keep his province in as good humor as possible. Here was a prisoner who was causing unrest in the province—"He stirreth up the people." To have done the right thing by Jesus would have been to incense still further the feeling of the leaders against himself, a feeling which was running high. "I must be careful. I must play safe. I must look out for Number One. It is true the man is innocent, but these people must be placated." And so he sacrificed the truth upon the altar of his own self-interest.

And so do we. For Pilate's problem is really our problem. No one of us escapes it. Does ever a day go by in which Truth does not stand before us, even as did Christ before Pilate? What is our choice? The politician must often choose between truth and votes. What is his choice? The business man must on occasion choose between truth and some sharp business practice in which he can "make a killing." What is his choice? The racially privileged must choose between truth and the prejudices which bolster racial pride. What is his choice? The minister must sometimes choose between truth and the possibility of losing his popularity or his position. What is his choice? The nation must choose between truth and the policy which for the moment furthers its nationalistic or imperialistic ends. What is its choice? "Ah, Pilate, we condemn you because when Truth stood before you, you loved yourself, your position, your future security more than you loved Truth. Yet, who are we to condemn you? Is there a single day that passes but that Truth is nailed to some Calvary, not because we do not hear its call, but because, like you, we are not men enough to heed its challenge?"

The key to Pilate's character, and to ours also, is found in his conversation with Jesus: "To this end was I born, and for this cause came I into the world, that I should bear witness unto the truth. . . . Pilate saith unto him, What is truth?" What a picture this is! Let us look at these men and see what makes one man willing to sacrifice everything, even life itself, for the truth, while the other man says he does not know what truth is. What *in the light of the Cross* is the difference between a soul like Jesus, who "steadfastly set his face to go to Jerusalem," and an opportunist like Pilate, who knew not steadfastness?

For one thing, it is obvious that Jesus lived under the mastery of a great compulsion. The opportunist who plays fast and loose with the truth is like a weathercock: he veers with the wind; like a thermometer, he rises and falls with the temperature of his time. Such was Pilate. He was mastered by no great loyalty. No transcendent principle held sway over his life. But the man who stood before him was held within the grip of a great compulsion. It was at Caesarea Philippi, which marks the turning point of Jesus' ministry, that he became increasingly aware of this compulsion. There Peter made his great confession, "Thou art the Christ." After that, Jesus "began to teach them, that the Son of man must suffer many things, and be rejected of the elders, and of the chief priests, and scribes, and be killed, and after three days rise again." Suffering, rejection, death! Not a pleasing prospect. A rather doleful end for so vigorous and abounding a life. It displeased Peter, who "took him, and began to rebuke him, saying, Be it far from thee, Lord: this shall not be unto thee." His rebuke was unavailing. Great men are not usually deterred by the voices of caution. Their course is determined not by the set of the wind but by the set of their souls. "And he began to teach them, that the Son of man *must* ..."

The opportunist does not know that word. He has no deeper compulsion than his varying moods, his vagrant whims and wishes, his selfish, mercenary aims. He sees no transcendent light. Jesus, on the contrary, lived under the mastery of a great compulsion. The word "must" was frequently on his lips. "Wist ye not that I must be about my Father's business?" "I must preach the Kingdom of God." "I must work the works of him that sent me." "He must needs go through Samaria." "And other sheep I have: ... them also I must bring." It is of course easy to assume that this intense loyalty of Christ to the truth was not of his own choosing but that it was preordained that he should face the cross and be faithful unto death. From this point of view he really had no choice at all. I cannot accept this interpretation. His choice was a voluntary one. To speak of a voluntary compulsion is to voice a paradox. As a matter of fact, however, a man is always free to choose his compulsion. There is a certain mechanical view of Jesus' life and work which is distasteful and quite unconvincing. It robs his life of that freshness and spontaneity without which all results lose their significance. This is why Calvin's theory of predestination and its more or less modern equivalent, Watson's behaviorism, are so deadly. According to this point of view the act of Jesus in choosing the cross becomes of no more significance than the act of Pilate in choosing his popularity and prestige. Both men were simply automatons, mechanical puppets, staging a prearranged performance in response to the pull of some cosmic string. To accept that view is to deny life.

This obligation of Jesus was voluntarily chosen. He distinctly said of his life, "No man taketh it from me, but I lay it down of myself. I have power to lay it down, and I have power to take it again." If one does not concede that Jesus was exposed to all the hazards of a free choice and may have chosen some other way, some easier way, as many men similarly situated doubtlessly would have done, then his great "I must" loses its appeal. "I have a baptism to be baptized with; and how am I straitened till it be accomplished?" But that baptism was not thrust on a good-natured if unfortunate victim; it was rather the free choice of one who counted the cost and willingly paid the price. "He took the cup."

> They borrowed a bed to lay his head
>   When Christ the Lord came down;
> They borrowed the ass in the mountain pass
>   For him to ride to town;

But the crown that he wore and the cross that he bore
   Were his own—
The cross was his own.

Our actions must always be viewed in the light of the motives that prompt them. We cannot really evaluate what a man does until we know why he does it. Here is a man who must support his family because the law compels him. Here is another who just as truly must, because love impels him. One man must pay his debts because the state makes him. The other man must from an inner sense of honor. Both men are under compulsions, but it makes all the difference whence these compulsions come. One must because he has to, the other because he wants to. One does it reluctantly, the other joyously. One is compelled, the other impelled. It is the voluntariness of Jesus' cross that makes perennially appealing this beautiful tragedy. "O Love divine, that stooped to share . . . " Jesus then freely and voluntarily chose to stand by the truth at the cost of his life, and Pilate to betray the truth at the cost of innocent blood.

There is no more thrilling chapter in human history than that of the great souls who, incarnating Christ's spirit, have made similar choices. Consider two of them. Take for example John Huss as he stood before the Council of Constance. How easy it would have been for Huss to be an opportunist! That council was considered, from the point of view of its outward pomp and splendor, the most brilliant and imposing of the ecclesiastical assemblies of the Middle Ages. The pope and emperor are present, each with a numerous and dazzling following of officers and attendants. Before this outwardly impressive but inwardly perverted assembly Huss is brought. The council will gladly acquit him should he yield. One of the cardinals advises submission. "If you do this, you will best consult your safety and your standing." But to this brave Bohemian there are matters of greater moment than either his "safety" or his "standing." The cause of truth is at stake. He stands firm. His anchor holds amid the gales. He does not swerve from the path that conscience has made clear. He is no weak-kneed Pilate! Rather, he sends this letter to his friends in Bohemia: "I write this in prison and in chains, expecting tomorrow to receive sentence of death, full of hope in God that I shall not swerve from the truth, nor abjure errors imputed to me by false witnesses. . . . In the truth which I have proclaimed, according to the Gospel of Jesus Christ, . . . I will, this day, joyfully die." [3]

Or consider that glorious soul Savonarola, a majestic man who in his fearless devotion to truth towers like some great mountain peak above the petty, pompous dignitaries of his day. No stone was left unturned to silence this fearless preacher of Florence. Lorenzo the Magnificent was a tyrannous, cruel, and unprincipled man. Savonarola minced no words in exposing publicly through his sermons the character of Lorenzo, who thought he could silence him through flattery or bribery. But his rich and lavish gifts served only to increase the contempt in which Savonarola held him. Said he as the gifts came, "A faithful dog does not leave off barking in his master's defense because a bone is thrown to him." The pope succeeded no better

[3] William N. Schwarze, *John Hus,* pp. 124, 129, 135.

than the prince. He too tried flattery. He would silence this brave prophet by making him a cardinal. A Dominican was sent from Rome bearing the offer of the cardinal's purple. This influenced Savonarola no more than the costly gifts of Lorenzo. It only increased his indignation, since it was proof positive that the church was making traffic of what in theory at least was supposed to be a sacred office. He was so aroused that his only reply to the messenger was, "Come to my next sermon, and you shall hear my reply to Rome." And if the messenger came, this is what he heard during the Lenten sermons of 1496: "I desire neither hats nor mitres, be they great or small; I desire naught save that which thou hast given to thy saints; it is death; a crimson hat, a hat of blood that I desire." It is hard to read the story of the final condemnation of Savonarola by the Papal commissioners, those arrogant, cruel nobodies who sent him to the gallows, without being impressed with the sense of one's own unworthiness. "The Lord hath suffered so much for me," he said as he died.[4]

Ah! but men like that who, unlike Pilate, yield neither to flattery nor fear, who can neither be bought by the world's prizes nor intimidated by the world's threats, stand like beacon lights. They tower above the popes and emperors of that day as the Master towered above Caiaphas and Pilate! The only enduring values of life are the spiritual values. True greatness is not first of all a matter of position, power, wealth, or worldly acclaim. True goodness is greatness of soul. It springs from one's knowledge of and loyalty to the truth. It comes from finding the time-

[4] Pasquale Villari, *Savonarola's Life and Times*, pp. 130, 401, 757.

less amid the temporary, from devotion to the values that are transcendent, which moth and rust do not corrupt, nor thieves break through and steal. The glory that leads to the grave is the glory that was Pilate's—the opportunist who knew no loyalty stronger than that of self-interest. But the glory that was Christ's does not end with the grave. It begins there and goes beyond death to life eternal.

> And from the ground there blossoms red
> Life that shall endless be.

But look again at these two men. Whence the difference? Not only that the man who stands for the truth is under a compulsion the opportunist never feels, but his constraint springs from within and is not imposed from without. The opportunist is comparable to the old sailing vessels that had to hug the shore or keep to the shallows. They could not adventure into the deep but had to steer their course by the little certainties on the shore line that were always within sight and within reach. The invention of the compass, however, put something inside the ship which made it independent of the shore line. It could then launch out into the deep, adventure in dangerous waters, because it had that within which could be trusted to take it to the land on the farther shore. A man who in the presence of Jesus asks, "What is truth?" reveals that the light within him has become darkness.

In a certain sense, is not that the trouble with the world today? It is a world confused and bewildered. It is groping. The age in which we live is crying out for daring and courageous leadership. The waters near the shore, in which we have been traveling, are not deep enough to float the larger vessels which the ampler life of this ever-shrinking planet now makes imperative. For the world is much smaller than it ever was. By some strange paradox, the smaller the world becomes, the bigger our outlook needs to be. Larger spiritual understanding is the only antidote to the ever-shrinking planet on which we live, else increased proximity will mean increased peril. The little certainties by which we have been steering our course are no longer adequate. We need now to steer by larger certitudes. But only the Master will inspire this spirit. Pilate will not. Whenever a choice must be made between some large challenging truth which involves adventure and risk and some consideration which though petty offers immediate certainty, Pilate steers his course by the latter. And who of us does not? The choice which at the moment seems most profitable always seems more desirable than that which in the long run is right. So it still seems.

This matter is not theoretical or abstract; it is tragically vital and relevant. The nations are trying to make peace— a peace which appears to be an "open discord openly arrived at." Will the nations have enough imagination to realize that "peace is not the absence of war but the presence of justice"? Shall we have another peace of opportunism and expediency, the result of shortsighted and selfish greed, or a Christian peace in which principles, not miserable policies, predominate? The question, I repeat, is anything but a theoretical one. A peace based on expediency is no peace at all, only another armistice.

In a world like ours, few policies are in the long run so unsafe as those that make us play safe. As far as getting

103

us out of the woods goes, no path is so hopelessly wrong as that of opportunism, which exalts clever politics above principles and, to keep some small, selfish loyalty on the throne, puts a larger loyalty on the cross. The opportunist, like Pilate, takes the course which in the short run seems best and so betrays the truth, which in the long run is all that matters. To be loyal to the truth, then, is to experience truth within. If the light within is darkness, no light outside can illumine us.

Finally, let us observe that in this bewildered and bewildering age our main hope is in becoming more like Christ in our attitude to truth, and less like Pilate. As far as making any contribution to the problems of our life is concerned, Pilate the opportunist is, to use a slang expression, a "washout." He has nothing to offer us. In other words, our hope lies in the principles of religion, not the expediencies of politics.

This is evident when we consider our civilization. One of the outstanding facts about it is that though man has made such amazing progress with nature he has made so little progress with himself. He has made incredible advances in many sciences but is still the most awkward of amateurs in the science of human relations. Why is this? It is, I think, largely because when we deal with nature we know we are dealing with a dependable world. We can count on nature to make certain reactions under certain given conditions. If you mix two parts of hydrogen with one part of oxygen, you do not get water today, wine tomorrow, and lemonade the day after tomorrow. You always get water. Now of course in the science of human relations we do not expect nor need such rigid and unvarying reactions as we get from the physical sciences. Variations will always be present because of our differing personalities, idiosyncracies, temperaments, or what not. And yet I maintain that in important matters, involving as they usually do questions of right and wrong, truth and error, we need not be in doubt.

Consider for example the fact of war and peace. No one of us knows for sure whether or not there will be another war. Yet there should be no reason whatever for uncertainty. The nations have put their names to the Atlantic Charter and the charter of the United Nations. While these are not perfect instruments, if the signatories lived up to their commitments there could not be another war. "If"—that is the question. Will we?

The problem of mankind springs from man's moral undependability. We are never quite sure at what moment some policy of expediency will make shipwreck of our high resolves. Even now, despite our commitments to principles, we are carrying on our off-stage horse-trading policies. If another calamity overtakes us, it will be due to those back-door dealings which, in the light of world conditions, are exceedingly dangerous and incredibly stupid. Such policies indicate that we have many ideas but few ideals, that there are many pebbles on our beach but no celestial body that lifts the tide and calls to the deep that is in us. "The Son of man must ... "—not because it was popular or profitable, but because it was right. That compulsion is lacking in our policies, and without it we are as the blind leading the blind. The ditch is the inevitable end. The future for man will not be brighter until he is mastered by and gives more than lip allegiance to principles that transcend the miserable policies of opportunism.

Can it be that we are playing the part of the opportunist because we are unwilling to pay the price that living by principle demands? No! The way we lavish our life and substance in war proves that we are neither miserly nor cowardly when it comes to paying the price. The reason is more baffling—namely, that we seem to lack the moral discrimination or spiritual insight that reveals the values worth purchasing. We practice appeasement, compromise, and all sorts of opportunistic policies which inevitably, as history shows, involve us in war. Then we stop at nothing as far as paying the price goes. In other words, we are unwilling to sacrifice anything to prevent calamity but will sacrifice everything to survive it—a fact which speaks loudly of our moral befuddlement. This is why our Calvaries, though costly, are not redemptive, while the Cross of Christ is the symbol of salvation. The difference lies partly in the motives that sent him to the cross and the values for which he died. Strange that we become so emotionally stirred over the fact of Jesus' death yet seem indifferent to the values for which he died. Yet only as we begin to live for those values can we find salvation.

It is not only in international affairs, however, that policies of opportunism bring calamity. They work havoc too in our national life. Opportunistic policies, conceived in selfishness and carried out for greed and graft, are the big millstone about the neck of democracy. What a transformation would be wrought in government if it were more government by principle and less by "politics"! Politics as practiced by us has almost become a synonym for what is immoral and corrupt. Think of our democracy. Despite its obvious failures, it is vastly better than what the dictators had to offer, since democracy at its worst is to be preferred to dictatorship at its best. But is the democracy that we practice worth what we have spent to preserve it? I for one do not think so. As a matter of fact, democracy as we often practice it ought not under any condition to be preserved, for it is not really democracy. What we have suffered and sacrificed to preserve is the everlasting hope that we may yet make democracy work, that we may make democracy in reality what it is in fact—the finest form of government in the world. We are not really worthy of the freedom we possess. We revel in its privileges and shun its responsibilities. Hence our liberty becomes license. Undisciplined freedom leads to disaster. The first fatality of undisciplined freedom is freedom itself. Without "the disciplines of liberty," liberty is lost. No form of government therefore needs so much the compulsion of some great principle as does democracy.

This, however, is news to the average politician for whom in many instances politics is little more than a selfish and sordid game. We all agree with Edmund Burke's dictum that "all political power which is set over men ought to be in some way or other exercised ultimately for their benefit." Abraham Lincoln said the same thing somewhat differently when he spoke of "government of the people, by the people, and for the people." But for the most part this is not the government we have today. Rather it is government *of* the politician, *by* pressure groups, *for* some end which, more often than not, by no stretch of the imagination could be identified with the public good. Too often do party interests or regional interests or personal interests take precedence over the public welfare; thus is the truth in democracy betrayed. Lester Ward may not have been exaggerating too much when he said, "In politics, we are still in the stone age." To say this is not to be unmindful of the fact that there are in government service men of the highest principles, of unquestioned integrity and ability. They are our hope. It is the presence of such men that keeps our democracy from complete disintegration and decay. They are like the salt that has not lost its savor.

Our constant need then, internationally as nationally, is for men who in their attitude to truth are less like Pilate, the opportunist, and more like the Master—men who possess moral courage. We all admire courage. We pin our choicest medals on those who do acts of daring, risk life in scorn of consequence. But there is a type of courage which surpasses physical bravery, and which is rarer. It is moral courage. Peter was no coward physically. Once he drew a sword and singlehandedly attacked those who had come to arrest Jesus. Yet this brave man gave evidence of moral cowardice when he denied his Lord. Pilate was no coward physically. He was a strong, brave man who was not afraid to face the foe and no doubt would have led his legions into battle. But he was a moral coward. If one has to be a coward it is much better to be a physical coward than a moral coward; for the most important battles of life are often those fought not against flesh and blood but against the spiritual forces that beset us. We have won the second World War, but physical victory, indispensable though it be, is not in itself a guarantee of a better world.

The physical victory we won at the close of the first World War did not bring a better world. It did not because when we faced the real issues and problems following the war, the moral and spiritual problems of reconstruction, we were moral cowards. Selfishness, caution, expediency, and opportunism became the allies of our spirit; and they vanquished us. We were weighed in the balance and found wanting.

The call of this hour is for moral heroes. Without moral courage man marks time; he cannot move forward. The call of this hour is for men who love truth more than they do praise, love truth more than advancement, love truth more than prejudice and pride, love truth more than their nation—yea, more than they love themselves. The call of this hour is for men who, when Truth stands before them, even if it is bound and bleeding and spat upon, as was the Christ, will not send it to be crucified but will enthrone it—enthrone it even if in so doing they dethrone themselves.

Such men may be rare, but they are our saviors.

V

Secularism: *Herod*

THE INDIVIDUAL during Holy Week who best represents the spirit of secularism is Herod Antipas. He was the second son of Herod the Great, and is said to have inherited all his father's vices and none of his virtues. Herod the Great had three sons who held official political positions—Archelaus, Herod Antipas, and Philip. Archelaus ruled over Judea, Samaria, and Idumea; Herod Antipas over Galilee and Perea; while Philip's domain extended over the regions northeast of the Sea of Galilee. It is Herod Antipas, Tetrarch of Galilee, who now concerns us. His rule over Galilee extended from 4 B.C. to A.D. 39; consequently his reign covered the earthly life of Jesus. His appearances in the Gospels reveal him as a secularist par excellence.

There are three such appearances. In the first one he is breaking up a home. He had married the daughter of Aretas, an Arab king. The marriage pleased the emperor of Rome, to whom he owed his appointment, since it tended to establish friendly relations between Palestine and Arabia. But Herod meets Herodias, his brother Philip's wife, divorces his own wife, and marries Herodias, thereby incensing the Arabs.

In his second appearance he is host at what proves to be a voluptuous and murderous banquet. It is his birthday and he is celebrating with a vengeance. Around him are the elite of Galilee. Salome, the sixteen-year-old daughter

of Herodias by her former husband, dances so captivating-
ly that Herod promises to give her whatever she may request, even "unto the half of my kingdom." She seeks her
mother's advice, as a young girl might very well do in such
an emergency, and her mother suggests that she ask for
the head of John the Baptist. This strange request was
prompted by the fact that her mother bore a grudge against
the old prophet, who, like Elijah before him, was not
afraid to reprove royalty. "It is not lawful for thee to have
her," said John to Herod when he ran off with Herodias.
And Herodias had not forgotten the reproof. Even before
this incident, however, Herod had reason to wish John out
of the way. His preaching of the kingdom of God was especially dangerous now that the Arab world was angered
because of Herod's divorce of his Arab wife. Herod therefore had put John in prison, and now by Salome's request
he could put him permanently out of the way.[1]

In his third appearance Herod and Jesus stand face to
face. This was their first meeting, though undoubtedly
they had heard of each other. Herod may have heard of
Jesus through the wife of one of his officials, Joanna, who
had become a follower of Jesus. But he "heard of him"
also through his own conscience. He apparently had enough
conscience left to be disturbed in his sober moments by
his murder of John the Baptist. When he heard of the
fame of Jesus, who at that time had a large following, he
concluded that Jesus was John the Baptist risen from the
dead. He tried therefore to put an end to Jesus as he had

[1] Some scholars maintain that the Salome incident is legendary. They
claim that the murder of the Baptist by Herod was due solely to the
danger of insurrection. See Clarence Tucker Craig, *The Beginning of
Christianity*, p. 74.

to John, and might have succeeded had not Jesus moved away beyond his reach. Jesus, however, sent a message to Herod. "Go, . . . tell that fox. . . ," he said. By the designation "fox" he might have been thinking either of Herod's cleverness or blood-thirstiness—or both. Herod was well supplied with both. Now Jesus and Herod stand face to face. The thoroughgoing secularist, gay man of the world that he is, stands in the presence of the Master. His actions and reactions are illuminating. Let us briefly consider them.

The first reaction of Herod, the secularist, was a frivolous one—he wanted Jesus to entertain him. We read: "And when Herod saw Jesus, . . . he hoped to have seen some miracle done by him." He wanted Jesus, like some clever magician, to pull a rabbit out of the hat. The secular mind may become so superficial that entertainment or amusement, particularly the type that is sensational, becomes its main fare. Herod's second reaction was flippant curiosity. We read: "Then he questioned with him in many words." There is a kind of earnest and wistful curiosity which is the key to truth, the gateway to wisdom. That there was nothing earnest or reverent about Herod's questions is evidenced by the fact that Jesus completely ignored them, which was an attitude he seldom assumed. Herod's third reaction was ridicule. "And Herod . . . set him at nought, and mocked him, and arrayed him in a gorgeous robe, and sent him again to Pilate." [2] We can understand the man who says: "I have no time for the Christian religion, I am too preoccupied. Its claims may be true

[2] Luke 23:11.

112

but I am too busy to consider them." We can sympathize with the man who says, "I do not believe in the Christian religion. Its beliefs and insights, though beautiful, are in my judgment unreal." But Herod's reaction was neither of these. He just made fun of the sacred—ridiculed it. In that act secularism strikes bottom; it can hardly sink lower.

Secularism then had its part in the crucifixion of Jesus. It has been an avowed enemy of Christianity ever since, being one of the formidable foes that Christianity confronts today. Herod represents the secular spirit at its lowest and worst. He was coarse, vulgar, licentious, cruel. There is enough of Herod's spirit in our age, to be sure, yet it must not be thought that all secularists are like Herod. The secularist may be refined, coldly respectable, and even well-behaved.

Our modern culture has become so prevailingly secularized that most of us do not realize how secularized it has become. If one of our Pilgrim fathers were ushered in upon the modern scene the fact would not escape him, for he would have known our culture when its presuppositions and scale of values were different from now. God said to Moses: "The place whereon thou standest is holy ground." It is not easy to find holy ground today. Harry Emerson Fosdick once said that holy ground was the scarcest piece of real estate in America.

And yet the idea of the holy has never been completely lacking from the human consciousness. In primitive society it is present in taboos. Some things are taboo—one stands in awe of them, they are sacred. This same idea, of course, occurs frequently in the Bible. There are sacred places like Mount Sinai, sacred objects like the Ark, sacred days like the Sabbath. In these and other ways the idea of the holy was kept in the consciousness of men. That idea, however, has been losing its hold under the rising tide of the religion of secularism. For secularism is a religion. Like all historic religions it has its devotees and disciples, its beliefs and assumptions. Indeed, it even has its rituals and its fellowships, and is perchance the religion from which Christianity has most to fear. For the greatest opposition to Christianity today comes not from the non-Christian religions but from secularism, which like the termite undermines the foundations of all religions. Let us then *in the light of the Cross* note the contrast between the religion of secularism and our historic faith.

For one thing, secularism is a man-centered religion, while Christianity puts God at the center. Secularism is not playing games or going to the movies on Sunday; these are merely some of its results. John Bennett describes secularism as life organized apart from God, just as though God did not exist. Above and beyond all this phenomenal world, our fathers envisioned an invisible world of spiritual realities. They were sure of this transcendent world. It was as real to them as that world which was amenable to their sense perceptions. They profoundly believed in God, as is evident from their culture, which was built about him.

Take the Middle Ages, for example. No doubt much can be said against the Middle Ages. It was a period when superstition and dogmatism ran high. But at least one great tribute can be paid to this period—its whole cultural life was centered around its faith in God. Hence the culture of the Middle Ages was an integrated, unified culture. The pride of its architecture was not the Empire State Build-

ing, symbol of our industrial prowess, but the cathedrals
—"the Bible in stone," as they have been called, symbols
of the greatness and the glory of God. This was equally
true of art. One has only to walk through the Uffizi Gal-
leries of Florence or stand before any of the great master-
pieces of the Old World to see how God-centered its
art was. Its music, too, was almost exclusively religious:
Alleluia, Gloria, Kyrie Eleison, Credo, Agnus Dei, Mass,
Requiem. And literature also. The influential books in
those days were not *Anthony Adverse, Gone with the Wind,*
or *Forever Amber,* but books like Augustine's *City of God,*
Dante's *Divine Comedy,* Thomas à Kempis' *Imitation of
Christ.* One could go on, but enough has been said to show
that the prevailing mark of the Middle Ages was its God-
centered culture. Above and beyond the seen and sensory
world men envisioned the transcendent, eternal world, and
even as the moon lifts the tide, so these heavenly realities
reached down into and radically influenced the nature of
all culture patterns. Such was the God-centered culture.
The place whereon it stood was holy ground.

It is hardly necessary to point out the difference between this culture and modern culture. Modern culture
lacks height and depth; it is too largely a flat reflection of
modern life. Now, to be sure, culture should reflect life,
but there is a flat reflection and there is also a reflection
which has depth and height. A mirror reflects the face of
the one who looks into it. A pool, too, reflects the face, but
more, it reflects the stars. By and large, modern culture is
like looking into a mirror. One sees one's self, but little
that transcends the self. There are notable exceptions;
but, by and large, when we read modern literature, hear

115

modern music, and see modern art, we are brought into touch with much that is crude, depressing, distorted, discordant, if not positively ugly. Medieval culture, too, reflected the life of its day, but it was not a flat reflection. It was a reflection that had some height and depth. It was the reflection not of a man who beholds himself in a mirror and, unfortunately, does *not* forget what manner of man he is, but of one who sees himself in the light of that which transcends the self, in the light of the Infinite. It is the lack of that element that makes modern culture flat and causes it to turn stale so soon. Modern culture lacks the sense of the holy. It does not know that the place whereon it stands is holy ground.

What brought about this shift from a God-centered to a man-centered culture; what blotted out the stars? There are no doubt many answers to that question, but I wonder if they do not come to this: everything has contributed to the growing sense of the power and self-sufficiency of man. For, you see, since secularism is a man-centered religion it must assume the self-sufficiency of man. Here again it stands in clear-cut contradistinction to historic Christianity. Historic Christianity maintains that man is not self-sufficient—"Who is sufficient for these things?" asks Paul, and answers, "Our sufficiency is of God." But secularism acts as though man were quite sufficient unto himself. The industrial revolution and the astonishing progress of science have contributed much to the illusion of human self-sufficiency.

There are two ways in which our scientific progress has misled us. For one thing, it bequeathed to us the belief in automatic progress which was so naïvely accepted by nineteenth-century thinkers. Progress, wrote Herbert Spencer, "is due to the working of a universal law; . . . in virtue of that law it must continue until the state we call perfection is reached. . . . Thus the ultimate development of the ideal man is logically certain—as certain as any conclusion in which we place the most implicit faith; . . . so surely must the things we call evil and immorality disappear; so surely must man become perfect." [3] It is difficult to imagine so sane and serious a student as Spencer writing such nonsense. He made his great mistake, of course, by taking evolution from the realm of biology and applying it to the social sciences. Many moderns have apparently done likewise. They have regarded science as an escalator: all we have to do is to get on, then the escalator does the rest. But something is radically wrong with that assumption. It is not true. That stupid superstition of automatic progress should be dead now, with no hope of resurrection.

Another way in which science has unwittingly misled us is that it has so immeasurably increased the power of modern man. The giants that the spies saw when they viewed the Promised Land or that Gulliver encountered in his travels are as nothing compared to modern man equipped with the techniques and tools of modern science. Science has made modern man more powerful than any giant of history or fiction. "The inventor of the first motor engine," writes Alan C. Bouquet in *The Christian Religion and Its Competitors Today,* "need not have been a militant atheist. But the enlargement of man's physical organs due to applied science (which has almost literally given

[3] *Social Statics,* pp. 78-80.

117

him new eyes, ears, arms and legs) has resulted in making
his spiritual institutions seem too small." It has been estimated that in the year 1800 there was only about a hundred thousand horsepower at work, and this largely animal power, to supplement human muscle in doing the
work of civilization. At the beginning of the year 1945
science had harnessed over a billion horsepower. Science
has deluged us with a vast amount of new and varied gadgets which preoccupy our attention as surely as a nursery
full of toys does the attention of a child. In these ways then
science has increased our sense of self-sufficiency. So Edwin
Markham in "Earth Is Enough" writes:

> We men of earth have here the stuff
> Of Paradise—we have enough!
> We need no other stones to build
> The stairs into the Unfulfilled—
> No other ivory for the doors—
> No other marble for the floors—
> No other cedar for the beam
> And dome of man's immortal dream.
> Here on the paths of every-day—
> Here on the common human way—
> Is all the busy gods would take
> To build a Heaven, to mold and make
> New Edens. Ours the task sublime
> To build eternity in time! [4]

That poem is admirable in its appeal to industry, courage,
and effort, an appeal which Christianity heartily endorses.
But the poem rests upon a fallacy. From "earth is enough"
the next step is "man is enough." The poet's view is whol-

[4] Used by permission.

ly horizontal. In truth earth is not enough, nor is man enough.

Let us now look at some of the inherent weaknesses and inadequacies of the religion of secularism. For one thing, it provides no organizing center for life. This is evidenced from our secularized culture, which lacks moral cohesion. The only word that I can use to describe some modern symphonies is "episodic." There are pretty little phrases here and there, but nothing ties them together. At the close of a modern symphony one sometimes feels like asking, "So what?" The symphony evidently lacks the cohesive power of some great compulsion that binds it together and makes it say something. That is more or less typical of our culture. There is nothing in which it coheres, nothing that holds it together. It is like a wheel without a hub—the spokes hang at loose ends. Our secular culture is a fragmentary culture. In fact, one reason why our civilization has been going to pieces is that it is a thing of pieces. "Gather up the fragments," said the Master; but secularism has no container big enough to hold them.

See how fragmentary our culture is! "Art for art's sake," we say. This spoke we have pulled from the hub. There is little doubt that technically some modern artists are just as great as the masters. But great art needs more than great technique. It needs a great motive, a great soul. It needs some sense of the divinity that lies in and behind all beauty. Charles Kingsley said: "Never lose an opportunity to see anything beautiful. Beauty is God's handwriting." But the secularist does not so regard it. To him beauty has little or no objective validity. It is largely subjective. Rodin, speaking of sculpture, said that

119

the mature artist should aim "to express not his own feeble or defective emotions, but his conception, his apprehension of . . . reality, felt through his emotions—that is the object of his search." If so much of modern art has declined into triviality it is largely because the artist treats beauty as though it were scarcely more than an idea with which he toys, a medium for expressing his individuality, with all the eccentricities, abnormalities, and distortions which his individuality may possess.

And so with other matters. Consider education. We have pulled that out of the hub, too. The secularization of modern education is one of the disturbing facts of our culture. To our fathers religion, morality, and knowledge were all of a piece. But knowledge is no longer a part of the trinity; it has seceded from the union. The Christian church played a leading role in the early educational adventures of our country. Our first colleges were all founded by the church. "Every one of the nine colleges in colonial times was founded with a view to supporting the claims of the Christian faith." The earliest of them, Harvard, was named for its initial benefactor, the Rev. John Harvard. The main objective of this college seems to have been "the preparation of ministers who would defend and propagate particularized religious doctrine." [5] It is rather a far cry from that to the report of the Harvard Committee on General Education in a Free Society. Says this committee, in part: "We did not feel justified in proposing religious instruction as a part of the curriculum. . . . We must perforce speak in purely humanistic terms, confining ourselves to the obligations

[5] From *Making the Gospel Effective,* ed. William K. Anderson, p. 113.

of man to himself and to society." [6] To use as a reason for omitting religious instruction the necessity of "confining ourselves to the obligations of man to himself and to society" is to reveal either an astonishing blind spot or surprising ignorance of the true nature of the Christian religion. Actually it would be hard to find two better reasons for its study than precisely those for which this committee has deemed it wise to omit it. The inadequacy of secularized culture was pointed out by Harvard's professor of the history of science, who has said that science has never been more necessary than today, nor less sufficient, and that in the future it will become more and more necessary and more and more insufficient.

What is true of education is true of other phases of our culture. It is true of business—we have pulled that spoke out of the hub, too. "Business is business," we say. We tend to act as though business were not a part of something bigger than itself, involved in all the moral and ethical relationships which characterize the dealings of people with each other, but a game, sometimes a sordid one, to be played without reference to the moral principles of God. All aspects of our culture, then, instead of being means to an end which transcends them are made ends in themselves. Our secular culture lacks unity. It is a thing of pieces and so it goes to pieces. That well-disciplined soul, the late William L. Sullivan, writes in his autobiography, *Under Orders*: "So at the end of the long journey I have come to this: the first article of my creed is that I am a moral personality under orders." The trouble with secularism

[6] From *The Christian Century*, Jan. 23, 1946, p. 109.

is that, as in the case of fascism, nazism, and communism, it too is the ultimate. There is no one from whom it takes orders; no light shines upon it from a transcendent realm. It lacks the cohesion which only comes when one has found a master.

But it lacks not only cohesion. Our secular culture also lacks meaning. This characteristic of secularism is the oft-repeated verdict of the secularists themselves. They say it in novels, in books on psychology and philosophy. They say it whenever they have a chance. The secularist never tires of telling us, *ad nauseam*, how utterly meaningless and vain life is. A typical prophet of this school, who may be selected to speak for all the rest, is the late Theodore Dreiser. He wrote: "I find life to be not only a complete illusion or mirage . . . but the most amazing fanfare of purely temporary and, . . . in the main, clownish and ever ridiculous interests that it has ever been my lot to witness. . . . As I see him, the unutterably infinitesimal individual weaves among the mysteries a floss-like and wholly meaningless course—if course it be. In short, I catch no meaning from all I have seen, and pass quite as I came, confused and dismayed." [7] And Theodore Dreiser, I repeat, is not a voice crying in the wilderness but part of a vast chorus. Life means nothing—nothing whatsoever. That is the verdict of the secularist on secularism. "Vanity of vanities; all is vanity."

The reason for this verdict is not hard to find. It is the inevitable conclusion of the secularist's premises. For if when a man looks at the world he sees nothing but a flat reflection of himself, if there be no sky above him, no

[7] Quoted in H. G. Leach, *Living Philosophies*, pp. 57, 74.

intelligence, purpose, or love beyond his own in this vast universe, then he is what Goethe called "a troubled wanderer upon a darkened earth." The thoroughgoing secularist not only denies that moral values have reference to anything beyond themselves but he denies that they have any unique significance at all. He not only severs morality from its superhuman source in God but "debunks" it and robs it of its ultimate meaning.

The personal and social effects of severing morality from its divine moorings are far-reaching. As far back as history goes, morals and religion have been in some way related. To primitive peoples right conduct was invariably regarded as a way to win the favor of the gods, and evil conduct, their displeasure. "Against thee, thee only, have I sinned," said the psalmist when he broke a moral law. If people believe that morality has no sanction apart from man and society, morality will lose its compulsion and become a matter of convention rather than conviction. If man made these moral laws there is no good reason why man cannot repeal or break them. And that is the crowning proof of the meaninglessness of a secular culture.

But the religion of secularism reveals its most arid and barren nature in the third aspect of its character: not only is it fragmentary, and by its own verdict ultimately meaningless, but in addition it lacks redemptive power. There simply is nothing within secularism that can redeem man. In 1939 there was a World's Fair in New York City. Nations from all over the world sent their exhibits, and hundreds of thousands from all parts of the world came to see them. The exhibits were amazing; one stood astonished before the well-nigh incredible scientific achievements of man. Scarcely, however, had the fair started than something else started: a war in Europe—a war which proved to be long, bloody, and costly; a war in whose raging fires some of the bravest and best of our men and choicest of our treasure have been alike consumed; a war from the material and spiritual dislocations of which it will take generations to recover. But what was there in all this astonishing mechanical achievement that could of itself reach down and touch the roots of war and lift man above its ravages? Little, if anything. On the contrary, what actually happened was that this mechanical achievement was turned against us to hasten our destruction.

At the heart of our secular culture then there is, says Pitirim A. Sorokin in *The Crisis of Our Age,* a "central self-contradiction. This consists in the fact that *our culture simultaneously is a culture of man's glorification and of man's degradation."* The great achievements of our secular culture seem of themselves as impotent to cure the ailments of a sick world as the application of vaseline might be in removing a tumor. That needs deep surgery. But there is nothing deep about secularism. It wears its heart on its sleeve. It has no moral resources for man's moral ills.

Despite all the natural and social sciences at our disposal, we are unable either to control the socio-cultural processes or to avoid the historical catastrophes. . . . On the eve of war most of the sciences were forecasting peace; on the eve of economic crash and impoverishment, "bigger and better" prosperity; on the eve of revolutions, a stable order and streamlined progress. . . . No better evidence of the nemesis of one-sided sensory truth is needed.[8]

[8] Sorokin, *op. cit.,* pp. 130-31.

And the late **H. G.** Wells's jeremiad is much worse:

> Our world . . . is like a convoy lost in the darkness on an unknown rocky coast with quarreling pirates in the chartroom and savages clambering up the sides of the ships to plunder and do evil as the whim may take them. Mind near exhaustion still makes its final futile movement toward that way out or around or through the impasse. . . . The writer is convinced that there is no way out or around or through the impasse. It is the end.[9]

What are we going to do about this great rival of Christianity? It is obvious that if there is an answer to secularism the church must find it; indeed, the church has it and must give it. Those were discerning words written some five years ago by the editor of *Fortune*: "There is only one way out. . . . The way out is the sound of a voice, not our voice, but a voice coming from something not ourselves, in the existence of which we cannot disbelieve . . . . Without it we are no more capable of saving the world than we were capable of creating it in the first place." [10] Surely it is not too much to say that no institution on earth is so fitted to mediate that voice as is the Christian church. It was of the fellowship of the church that John was writing when he spoke of being "born, not of blood, nor of the will of the flesh, nor of the will of man, but of God." No wonder responsible men look to the church as the institution that should mediate God's will and way to a perplexed world. What then can the Christian church say or do?

I shall not attempt to give an adequate answer but

[9] Cleveland *News,* Nov. 5-6, 1945.
[10] *Fortune,* January, 1940, pp. 26-27.

merely to indicate two lines along which it will be found—
one in the realm of belief, the other in the realm of action.
In the realm of belief, the church must be the church. It
was a wise theologian who once observed that wherever
you find the church, you will also find a little of the world.
But the more of the world there is in the church, the less
can the church help the world. Herein of course lies the
crux of the difficulty. The sad truth is that not only have
art, business, education, and other aspects of our culture
been secularized, but the church itself has not escaped. It
has fallen to aping secular society, and a church which is
part of the disease cannot provide the cure. The transforming influence of the early church on the life of its age was
singular indeed. To be a Christian then was to be different.
Paul voiced the principle of nonconformity with secularism when he wrote to the Romans: "Be not conformed
to this world: but be ye transformed by the renewing of
your mind, that ye may prove what is that good, and accept-
able, and perfect, will of God." The early church did not,
putty-like, adjust itself to the standards or patterns of its
secular surroundings. It was a worthy successor of Isaiah's
"remnant." It bore witness, by its life, to a transcendent
truth, in the light of which its own life and that of the
pagan age were brought to judgment. A church that is the
echo of the world's voice, prating its prejudices, following
its foibles, mimicking its methods, will not influence the
world. The church of the living God is not supposed to
be an echo of the world's voice but the voice of God to
the world.

As the church overcomes the evils of secularism within
its own fellowship it will be able correctly to diagnose the

human situation. Despite the sophisticates who tell us that the major problem of life is economic, political, or something else, the church will insist that man's primary problem, from the day of Eden until now, is basically moral and spiritual. Science can never solve the major problems of human life, for the simple reason that they are not scientific but human problems, and every human problem is ultimately a moral and spiritual problem. This is the Christian insight and it is unquestionably the right one. Is not this in itself of tremendous significance, since the first step in effecting any cure is arriving at a correct diagnosis of the disease? Our illness is fundamentally moral and spiritual. I suppose one reason why the secularist avoids the correct diagnosis of our condition is that he knows full well that once you admit that the human problem is essentially a moral and spiritual one, you are bound to admit also that the solution will not be anything novel or startling. Science has given the modern prodigal, be he prodigal son or prodigal world, speedier methods of destruction. But science has not and never can give him speedier methods of spiritual regeneration. One would have a right to be suspicious of any analysis or proffered solution of the human situation that was new or original. We do not get into our predicaments by new roads, nor out of them either.[11]

I suspect that many moderns are expecting some clever person to invent or discover a royal road to salvation, some agency that in the moral realm will be the eqivalent of an

[11] I am thinking now of pure science. Admittedly, in the field of the social sciences—psychology, for instance—there is much that has proved helpful in the cure of souls.

elevator in the physical realm, which at the push of a button will lift us to a higher plane *with no effort to ourselves*. There will never be any such invention in the moral realm. The way to the far country is the same old one of self-will, and the way back the same old one of penitence and discipline. Descartes once said, "If it should ever prove possible to find some means of making men gentler and wiser than heretofore, I believe that means will be found in medicine." It would indeed be wonderful if we could cure our spiritual ills by taking a pill, but since the diagnosis shows that our ailment is not physical, physical remedies will not avail.

It is not enough to insist, however, that our problem is moral and spiritual. The church will proclaim that moral and spiritual ideals mean little if divorced from the sustaining power of a great faith.[12] The Ten Commandments were rooted in faith in God; Sinai thundered God's presence. The Sermon on the Mount divorced from Jesus' faith in the living God would be little short of fantastic nonsense. "The Jesus way of life" separated from his faith is one which he would never have discovered. Even the values of our culture which the secularist espouses have their roots in some transcendent faith. Democracy is the fruit of faith. Its cornerstone, the worth of individual man, is a Christian postulate which derives from man's worth to God as taught by Jesus. Nietzsche was right when he said, "The democratic movement is the inheritance of the Christian movement"; or as Glenn Frank puts it, "Democ-

---

[12] This aspect of the matter has been discussed with clarity and conviction by D. Elton Trueblood in his book *The Predicament of Modern Man,* chap. iii.

128

racy cannot survive apart from a spiritualized religion that preserves in a man a sense of the sanctity of the individual human spirit." We may say without discrediting the contribution of the Greeks, that modern democracy is the fruit of which the Christian tradition is the roots. This fact, however, seems to escape completely the modern secularist. The truth of the matter is that the great ethical values which have grown out of a profound faith in God will not survive if severed from their historic rootage. Professor Trueblood refers to our civilization as a "cut flower civilization." We pluck the flowers but ignore the roots that nurtured them into bloom. And I may add that cut flowers will fade, never mind how many aspirin tablets one puts in the water.

The church's answer, however, lies not only in the field of faith but of action also. It was said of the Master: "In him was life; and the life was the light of men." The transforming power of Christ in human hearts and history does not come just from his words—other seers have spoken wisely and well—but from his life. One unique fact about Jesus is that he *was* what he said—*"the life* was the light of men."

> And so the Word had breath, and wrought
> With human hands the creed of creeds
> In loveliness of perfect deeds,
> More strong than all poetic thought.

One great weakness of the Christian church is that in the realm of belief we strut, while in the realm of action we straddle. Christianity is exhaustively studied but sparingly lived. Long ago one of the Church Fathers com-

129

plained: "For the Gentiles when they hear from our mouth the oracles of God, marvel at them for their beauty and greatness; then, when they discover that our works are not worthy of the words which we speak, forthwith they betake themselves to blasphemy, saying that it is an idle story and a delusion." [13] "Take with you words," said Hosea, but the words that help and heal are those that bear witness to reality: "We speak that we do know"; "The words that I speak unto you, they are spirit, and they are life." The words that are life-giving are the ones that grow out of life as a tree from the soil.

Do you suppose, for example, the church can be much help in pointing the way through our racial problems when its own fellowship denies its gospel? "Physician, heal thyself." How much weight do you think the voice of the church carries as it pleads for unity among the nations when its own divided life belies its plea? "Physician, heal thyself." An ounce of example here would be worth a pound of profession. T. R. Glover, in accounting for the victory of Christianity over paganism in the early centuries, said the Christians "outlived" the pagans. Christians still could—"the life was the light." And that is one light that can never be put out.

[13] II Clem. 13:3.

VI

Militarism: *The Soldiers*

IN THE GOSPEL according to Mark we read: "And the soldiers led him away into the hall, called Praetorium; and they call together the whole band. And they clothed him with purple, and platted a crown of thorns, and put it about his head, and began to salute him, Hail, King of the Jews! And they smote him on the head with a reed, and did spit upon him. . . . And when they had mocked him, they took off the purple from him, and put his own clothes on him, and led him out to crucify him." [1] The soldiers taunted, mocked, and finally crucified Jesus.

Of course in a sense they were not to be blamed. They were but carrying out orders. To obey unquestioningly and promptly is the first duty of a soldier. It has been suggested that when Jesus prayed, "Father, forgive them; for they know not what they do," he was thinking of the Roman legionaries, whose duty it was to carry out the orders of crucifixion. At any rate, the soldiers crucified Jesus. They bound him to the cross, spiked his hands and feet, and pierced him with a spear. They were representatives of the military and may well be taken as symbols of the militarism which from that day to this has taunted, mocked, and crucified the Son of God afresh. It is not my purpose, however, to discuss the evils of war, which are too obvious to be recounted, but rather to remind ourselves that the cause of peace is the task of not just the diplomat or states-

[1] Mark 15:16-20.

man but of people like you and me, and that we cannot evade it.

No speech of Abraham Lincoln is so well-known as his Gettysburg Address. People had come to the national cemetery at Gettysburg, Pennsylvania, to listen to Edward Everett, the great orator. His two-hour oration, so widely acclaimed by the newspapers, was soon to be forgotten. Lincoln's address was to become immortal. In part he said: "It is for us the living, rather, to be dedicated here to the unfinished work which they who fought here have thus far so nobly advanced. It is rather for us to be here dedicated to the great task remaining before us,—that from these honored dead we take increased devotion to that cause for which they gave the last full measure of devotion —that we here highly resolve that these dead shall not have died in vain."

As one reads again those words of Lincoln, he thinks of the words of the unknown author of the epistle to the Hebrews, which Abraham Lincoln, familiar with the Bible as he was, no doubt knew: "These all died in faith, not having received the promises, but having seen them afar off. . . . God having provided some better thing for us, that they without us should not be made perfect." "They without us should not . . ." said the author of Hebrews. "It is for us the living, . . . that we here . . . resolve that these dead shall not have died in vain," said Lincoln.

One of the great tragedies of war is that the dead have so often died in vain—not wholly so, but largely so. The first World War was fought to make the world safe for democracy. It did not; it set the stage for dictatorship. It was to be a war to end war. It did not; it unwittingly sowed the seeds which twenty-five years later we harvested in the most colossal war in human history. From this point of view it seems as though the dead did die in vain. The second World War was fought for the "four freedoms." It was fought to eliminate tyranny and lay the foundations of the world in international co-operation and justice, and so in peace. Will these aims be realized, or will these dead, too, have died in vain? It is for us the living to answer this question. The dead cannot answer it.

Let us try to answer it in two ways: first, by deciding why we must abolish war; and second, by considering some possible steps toward its abolition. We must abolish war because it makes a mockery of Christianity. It taunts, mocks, and crucifies the Master, as did the soldiers long ago. One does not need to be an absolute pacifist to know that war is absolutely unchristian. It denies every truth that Christianity affirms. Christ's most daring assumption is that the human race is a family under the universal fatherhood of God. War converts the universal Father into a tribal deity, and makes utter shipwreck of the brotherhood of man. Wrote Paul: "For he is our peace, who hath made both one, and hath broken down the middle wall of partition between us." The walls that Christ would break down, war builds up and reinforces with tons of steel. Christ's great goal was the kingdom of God, a universal kingdom of righteousness, love, and good will. Wars are fought for the particular kingdoms of man, and, even when fought for righteous ends, they seldom promote righteousness. For the spirit of self-righteousness which invariably pervades the victor makes difficult if not impossible the spirit of

133

justice, to say nothing of mercy, in dealing with the vanquished.

"Not by might, nor by power, but by my spirit, saith the Lord of hosts." "The fruit of the Spirit is love, joy, peace, longsuffering, gentleness, goodness, faith. . . ." The fruit of the spirit is never harvested by the weapons of the flesh. These weapons can stem the tide of evil, but cannot remove evil. The armies of the United Nations stopped the forces of tyranny and turned them back upon themselves, but only the weapons of the spirit can lay the foundations of a better world. J. N. Darling some time ago published a prophetic cartoon. It showed an American soldier with an ax, about to chop down a huge, terrifying tree labeled "World War II." Not far from him was a group of civilians and diplomats, one of whom held a portfolio of postwar peace plans. The soldier was saying, "I'll cut down the tree; but God help us if you don't prevent its sprouting again." [2] The soldier cannot do the constructive work of peace, yet that work must be done. For the alternative is still Christ or Mars.

This alternative has been sharpened and the choice made more urgent by virtue of the changed nature of modern war, which is the second reason why we must abolish it. Consider some of these changes. For one thing, we can no longer localize war. Once we could, even as doctors do infection. A war could be fought in one part of the world while in the rest of the world business went on as usual. That day is done. All future wars, if such there be, will be global. Not only so, but we can no longer localize destruction. Once upon a time we could keep destruction in the

[2] *Missions*, November, 1945, p. 476.

front lines, but that day too has gone. In modern war the front line is a fiction. Our country has been involved in two world wars and each time destruction has been kept from our shores. But not again. If there be another war, no spot on earth will be safe. The entire planet will be "No Man's Land." The cities of America will be just as much in the war zone next time as Coventry, Cologne, London, Berlin, Tokyo, or Nagasaki were this time. Arthur H. Compton, the noted physicist, warns us that no city of over a hundred thousand population will remain an effective operating center after the first hours of the next war. In the second World War Japan was able to send her balloons as far east as Michigan. She was getting ready to send long-range one-way heavy bombers to attack our cities. Although her balloons did little damage, in the future, when loaded with atomic bombs, as of course they will be, her balloons and bombers will tell a different story.

The most radical change in war, however, has come from the release of atomic energy, which overnight has made war as we have known it, with its superfortresses, superdreadnaughts, lumbering tanks, and vast armies of marching men, all but completely obsolete. So much has been said and written about the atomic bomb that I suppose many people wish there might be a moratorium on its discussion. It is, however, a fact that the release of atomic energy has posed a terrific problem for mankind. No one knows this as well as do our scientists. Some of them have well-nigh become preachers. At any rate, they realize that science, far from being the messiah that the superficial had supposed it would be, bids fair to become our destroyer unless we can build up inner moral and spiritual controls.

The incredible power of the atomic bomb has brought about this awareness. The two bombs that were dropped on Japan, amazingly destructive though they were, are now regarded as having been quite ineffective. As a matter of fact, we are told that only about one tenth of one per cent of their atomic charge was actually consumed by the atomic reaction. We are now being informed that one bomb would be sufficient completely to destroy the city of New York and every inhabitant of it. This, we are assured, is a "mathematical certainty." Indeed, one of our educators hazards the prediction that in fifty years we shall probably be able to start a chain reaction that could blow up the globe. And M. L. E. Oliphant, of the University of Birmingham, Britain's leading experimenter in atomic physics, has warned that atomic scientists are now able to produce an atomic poison gas which if used with an atomic bomb would kill every living thing within a radius of a thousand miles. This means that three bombs dropped at the proper spots could wipe out the entire population of the United States,[3] and these bombs, remember, will be transported by pilotless rocket planes which, as Norman Cousins says, "will be capable of hitting any specified target area in the world within the radius of a single mile." No wonder our great military leaders are speaking as they do.

General Dwight D. Eisenhower in his speech before the Congress in June, 1945, said: "Peace is an absolute necessity in this world. The nations cannot stand another world catastrophe of war." General Douglas MacArthur in his Tokyo Bay speech aboard the S.S. *Missouri,* on September

[3] *The Christian Century,* Dec. 5, 1945, p. 1341.

2, 1945, was even more specific. Said he: "The utter destructiveness of war now blots out the alternative. We have had our last chance. If we do not now devise some greater and equitable system Armageddon will be at our door. The problem basically is theological and involves a spiritual recrudescence and improvement of human character. . . . It must be of the spirit if we are to save the flesh."

This brings us to the question "How are we to eliminate this evil which not only denies our Christian insights but now bids fair to destroy the human race?" One answer is the United Nations. No wonder King George VI, in addressing the assembly of this organization at its first meeting in London, January 9, 1946, could say, "In the long course of history no more important meeting has ever taken place within its [London's] boundaries." We must face the disillusioning fact, however, that, essential and indispensable though the United Nations organization is, it cannot of itself bring peace. Political institutions cannot of themselves create unity. Nobody realizes this better than those who have been nearest to this organization. D. Elton Trueblood, church peace consultant at the San Francisco Conference, in an article published by the Canadian Conference of Christians and Jews in June, 1945, put the matter clearly when he said:

There is a realistic sense of the inadequacy of this or any other scheme. The men most responsible are not naive believers in the success of a printed document. When objectors point out that some particular dire eventuality might not be prevented by anything in the charter, the answer given is that, if there is a will to war on the part of the great powers, neither this nor any other document will avoid war. All that a system can do is to facilitate peace when a will to peace exists. . . . In short, the chief sponsors of the new system of world organization are disarmingly modest in their claims. They do not expect to produce a panacea.

This is simply another way of saying that if the charter of the United Nations works, *we* must work it. We cannot rest upon our oars as though an organization without our determined effort will bring us to our promised haven. "The foundation of peace lies in the hearts of men."

Let us then *in the light of the Cross* consider six steps which illumine the way to peace. They are steps which all Christians should take, because Christians have vastly more at stake in the cause of peace than do politicians or statesmen. In war the statesman is concerned primarily, if not exclusively, about his country. The Christian is concerned also about mankind. For while the Christian is loyal to his country, he professes a larger loyalty to the kingdom of God; he realizes that, regardless of who wins or loses in war, Christianity always stands to lose, since war completely denies the profoundest Christian insights. Not only, however, does the Christian have more at stake in war than the politician or statesman but, as I like to believe, he has more to contribute to the cause of peace. This is because in principle as a Christian he views the issues of war and peace above those areas of prejudice and bigotry which becloud the vision and befuddle the minds of those who lack the Christian perspective. Here then are some of the unique contributions which the followers of the Prince of Peace the world over, each in his own country, can make to the cause of peace.

For one thing, Christians can contribute the faith that peace is possible. We have no way of estimating the appalling drag that has handicapped the cause of peace because, even while we have been talking peace and planning peace, deep in our hearts we have sincerely doubted the possibility of peace. It is not hard to understand why we have doubted. Human history is so largely a record of wars and rumors of wars that periods of peace seem like mere interludes during which men catch their breath and sharpen their swords for the next conflict. So long have men dreamed of peace, and so often have their dreams ended in rude awakenings, that even now under our talk of peace there is heard the distant rumbling of cynicism. "You can't change human nature." "We have always had wars and we always will have wars." Yet the insight of Jesus is still true; it takes faith to remove mountains, especially the mountain of militarism. Nothing great is ever accomplished in an atmosphere of doubt, cynicism, or despair. "According to your faith be it unto you." Let all those who want peace believe that peace is possible. Then perchance these dead shall not have died in vain.

Again, Christians will understand, and help others to understand, that peace is not cheap. If peace could be had for nothing we should long since have had it. But peace is not cheap. No good or great value is ever cheap. There is a strange quirk in all of us—we think that good things are free or may be had for little or nothing. The story has it that a man stepped into a drugstore one Sunday morning shortly before eleven, placed a dime on the counter, and said to the druggist, "Will you please give me two nickels?" "Here they are," said the druggist, "and I hope you enjoy the sermon." So from the church on through the list we act as though good things could be had for little or nothing. This is of course a costly blunder. Like all good and great values, peace costs. It just happens that we have never been willing to pay the price. Jesus told a story once about a man seeking goodly pearls, who when he found one of great price sold all he had and bought it. The articles he sold were not rubbish; he sold pearls. He parted with pearls of lesser value in order to get the pearl of great price. On any count peace is a pearl of great price. But we cannot buy so great a pearl with rubbish. We shall have to part with some lesser pearls. Peace costs.

Think of what war costs. Take the second World War for example. We started out by sending fifty old destroyers to Britain. Then we began on "lend-lease," and after that we poured billions upon billions into the struggle, and millions of men. The cost was not limited just to our country; other countries bore similar costs. Actually, I do not believe it is possible to estimate what this war cost the world. We cannot adequately compute its drain on our civilization, material and spiritual. And yet we met this cost courageously. For war we give unstintingly, lavishly of our blood and treasure. When peace beckons we count each penny and squeeze it before we let it go. But peace will cost us something. It is said that the best things in life are free. This is true in the sense that no one has a monopoly on them, they are open to all; but not in the sense that they may be had without effort, discipline, or renunciation. Peace will cost, but war costs infinitely more.

"Wherefore do you spend money for that which is not bread? and your labour for that which satisfieth not?" [4]

In the third place, Christians are peculiarly fitted to help the nations cultivate the spirit of national self-criticism. There should be nothing inconsistent between loving one's country and being critical of one's country. They say that love is blind, but when love becomes so blind that it cannot distinguish between virtues and vices it is too blind. It is strange how we adopt a double standard of morality, one for the individual and one for the nation. The individual who swaggers and struts or pretends to be the greatest pebble on the beach we regard as an egotist or a fool. Yet this very arrogant, self-assertive spirit which we condemn in the individual we not only condone but often even admire in the nation. It is clearly evident, however, that this type of patriotism, which makes us regard everything American if one is an American, or everything British if one should be British, or French if one be French, as being "one hundred per cent," simply lacks reality. It is an expression of prejudice, not of truth. Jesus loved his country. He was at home in its literature. He knew and loved its great men—Abraham, David, Solomon, Elijah, Isaiah. Yet the Master was not unmindful of the shortcomings of his country. Once he wept over its capital city because it had fallen so short of its privileges and responsibilities. In the book of Hebrews we read of those who "desire a better country." No country, however, can become better save as its citizens recognize its shortcomings. It was because Jesus longed to see his coun-

[4] Isa. 55:2.

try a better country that he was conscious not only of its virtues but of its failings too.

Consider, for instance, the attitudes of two Japanese—Matsuoka and Kagawa. Said Matsuoka, in speaking of Japan: "Our mission is to rescue the human race from destruction and lead it to the world of light. We have a peerless tradition. Providence calls on Japan to deliver humanity from the impasse of modern material civilization." [5] So speaks a blind, bigoted nationalist to whom everything Japanese is "peerless." Contrast this with these words of Kagawa, the great Christian leader. After Japan started her unprovoked, aggressive war against China, Kagawa sent his now familiar letter to the Christians of China, a part of which reads: "Dear Brothers and Sisters,— I want to ask your pardon for my nation. Because of what we are doing, I cannot preach in the name of Christ. . . . Therefore pardon us, pardon me especially, because our Christian forces were not strong enough to get the victory over the militarists."

Now whom do we regard as the real patriot here—the man who is so blindly Japanese that everything concerning his country, even her utterly wicked war against China, is right and peerless, or the man who loves his country so much that he cannot condone or bless her evil ways? If Japan, and indeed all the nations, had had more patriots of the Kagawa type and fewer of the Matsuoka type, we should not have been involved in World War II. As Mazzini has said, "The honor of a country depends much more on removing its faults than on boasting of its qualities." If the nations can adopt this spirit of national self-

[5] Quoted by Upton Close, *Reader's Digest*, March, 1935, p. 114.

criticism, then perchance these dead shall not have died in vain.

Again, who are so well qualified as are Christians to help create a new concept of who our enemies really are? We came to regard the Germans and the Japanese as our enemies. We looked upon these human beings as the embodiment of all the ugliest traits of human nature. As we read and actually saw pictures of their amazing bestiality and depravity, we could hardly believe our eyes. They violated every rule of warfare. They stopped at nothing. They seemed neither to fear God nor to regard man. We called the Germans "Huns" or "Krauts," and the Japanese "Rats." (Incidentally, in this matter of atrocities our hands are far from clean.) And yet if we are going to have lasting peace we shall have to stop that sort of thinking. Rather we shall have to ask, "How did these people develop such cunningly brutal and beastly characteristics? Are they biologically a lower breed, or can it be that their social conditioning over many years, if not centuries, has made them what they are?" Many people, I know, will say that the Germans and the Japanese are by nature brutal and depraved. I do not share that belief. The Germans and the Japanese are human beings like the rest of us, whose minds and hearts have been poisoned and perverted by continuous and increasing doses of sociological and religious slush. The poor German youths who devastated Europe had never known or read anything but what had come from the distorted and depraved mind of Hitler. Indeed, long before that abnormal man appeared on the horizon, Germany had been under the heels of her misguided militarists, who for generations misled the Ger-

143

man people in a false sense of the glory of militarism as
the path to power and world domination. Helmuth von
Moltke, chief of the Prussian general staff, referred to war
as "a part of God's world order." In one of his letters,
written in 1880, he says: "Eternal peace is a dream, and
not even a beautiful one, and war is a part of God's world
order. In it are developed the noblest virtues of man,
courage and abnegation, dutifulness and self-sacrifice at
the risk of life. Without war the world would sink into
materialism." [6]

> Upon what meat doth this our Caesar feed,
> That he is grown so great?

That kind of meat!

And as to the Japanese, their case is even worse. Their
indoctrination in the myths of their divine ancestry and
racial superiority was thoroughgoing and complete. It
has been going on for hundreds of years. If, however, the
Germans and the Japanese had had another kind of indoctrination, they would have been an entirely different
kind of people. How can we doubt that? As a matter of
fact many Japanese Christians, far from sharing the fanatical ideas of their fellows, risked their lives after Pearl
Harbor to protect their American friends, the missionaries.
These same Christians are now saying that they are
genuinely grateful that Japan lost the war, since had she
won it there would have been no living with the military
who would have strutted and rattled their sabers as never
before. Similarly, many German Christians who escaped
Hitler's propaganda actually languished in concentration

[6]Quoted in Karl Liebknecht, *Militarism*, p. 23.

144

camps rather than submit to the Nazis. This goes to show that our real enemies were not the Germans and Japanese as such, but the perverted and distorted ideas that made them what they were. That is the truth in Paul's great insight that our wrestling is not against flesh and blood but against the spiritual forces of evil. And those forces of evil exist, mind you, not only in our "enemies" but in ourselves also.

Our enemy then, as our gospel rightly teaches, is not man as such but the evil in man. That is the real cause of war. This thought was well put by one of the boys of our church in a letter addressed to his mother while he was in the army of occupation in Germany:

They [the Germans] are our enemies, but outwardly at least they are just like anyone else. We've fought them so long and hard that I think we rather expected these people to be very different in their ways. But the kids play the same, and the older people are industrious in working in their gardens, etc. The little things we see are all like everything we've ever known: they sweep the same, wash their clothes the same, etc. But underneath it all lies the deep-seated penetration of the teaching of the Reich and the Nazi party.

A good analysis. The German people are the same, but underneath lies "the deep-seated penetration of the teaching of the Reich and the Nazi party"—only a different indoctrination.

Listen to the same truth expressed by the chancelor of the University of Chicago. In his V-E Day address at the university he said:

The peace of the world depends upon the restoration of the German and Japanese people. The wildest atrocity stories cannot alter the simple truths that all men are human, that no men are beasts, that all men are the children of God, that no men are irrevocably damned by God, and that all men are by nature members of the human community. These truths must dictate our attitude toward and decisions about the German and Japanese people. The misbehavior of an individual man, resulting from miseducation, misdirection or stress of circumstances, does not permit us to forget that he is a man or to treat him as a brute or to act like brutes ourselves. If we are going to have one good world, the Germans and the Japanese must somehow be incorporated into it. The basis of such incorporation must be justice and mercy.[7]

If any doubt remains that our real enemies are not people as such but the perverted ideas which make them dangerous, it should be dispelled by the fact that though the Germans are beaten, Germany is still a big problem. Moreover, should the ideas or spirit that made the Germans and Japanese a menace be adopted by any of our former allies, we should immediately regard them as our "enemies." If all who love peace see this clearly, then perchance these dead shall not have died in vain.

Another great contribution which Christians are peculiarly fitted to make to peace is that of helping the nations to disassociate the patriotic spirit from the military spirit. We must insist that it is patriotic to live for one's country —not only to die for it. It is tragic that patriotism should be so exclusively connected with war. Militarism has become inextricably tied up with our national traditions. It is imbedded in our song and story, to say nothing of our textbooks. Every British schoolboy knows the story of

[7] Robert Maynard Hutchins, "In the Name of Our Dead," *The Christian Century*, May 23, 1945.

Drake, who left his bowling on the Hoe to put to flight the Spanish Armada, as every American schoolboy knows the story of Bunker Hill. But are they familiar with the exploits of the great who followed peaceful pursuits? Patriotism, you see, has become "glorified violence." Our greatest monuments are always to the heroes of the battlefield. France built a great tomb for Napoleon. Close by is a relatively insignificant statue erected to Louis Pasteur. Napoleon was a military genius. Some of his predecessors and successors, the Nazis being the most recent, make it clear that the phrase "military genius" is often the polite equivalent for international gangster. At any rate, Napoleon left his trail of blood and destruction across Europe. Pasteur gave his life constructively to save men. Every one of us owes a debt to that great French chemist whose discoveries did so much for medicine, and so for mankind. But France does not regard the man who used his talents constructively for the glory of God and the service of man as on a par with the man who gloried in war and glorified it. France is no exception.

In saying that we should not identify the patriotic spirit with the military spirit, I do not mean to cast any aspersions whatsoever upon the brave men who die for their country. In fact, as I think of the men who died in the second World War, some of whom I knew and loved, I can find no word that can adequately express the gratitude, esteem, and affection in which we should and do hold them. It is rather *in behalf of them* that I say that, unless we are to continue sacrificing unborn generations upon the awful altar of war, we must recognize the patriotism and even heroism of

147

those who in times of peace constructively live for their country.

The results of failing to do this were evident during the second World War. We expected the men who stormed the beaches of Normandy, or broke the Siegfried Line, or stopped Von Rundstedt at the Battle of the Bulge, or struggled in the fiery hell which was Okinawa, to be brave, self-sacrificing—patriotic. But we seemed to apply a different standard to those of us at home. Here all too often selfishness rather than sacrifice was manifested: witness the black markets which flourished and the strikes, frequently unjustified, which withheld from those who were giving their lives the weapons necessary for their defense. In comparison with those of the men at the front, our motives were far from noble. But, you see, we at home did not need to be noble, for we were not in uniform and so did not have to be patriotic. We must be patriots at the battle front. We do not have to be at the home front. This is wrong. Those were brave words spoken by the Archbishop of Canterbury, William Temple, in *The Hope of a New World*. Said he: "It is easier to die for a cause than to live for it; for it means the setting aside of pleasure and self-interest in a host of little choices, where there is no glory, at least in men's eyes, on the one side, and no open shame on the other. Yet if life is to keep for us its dignity and value, we must find something to live and die for in peace as in war." If we cease to identify patriotism so exclusively with war, then perchance the dead shall not have died in vain.

Finally, we must strive to enlarge our concept of patriotism. Our patriotism must be less exclusive, more in-

clusive. Is not this the peculiar obligation of the followers
of him who, by his Cross, seeks to draw all men? It is interesting to see how the idea of patriotism has widened
out. The first patriot was the man who loved his family,
for in primitive society the family was the biggest unit.
Then the unit enlarged; it became the clan. And so the
true patriot was the man who was loyal not just to his
family but to the clan. The clan was later superseded by
the tribe, and the true patroit then became the man who
was loyal not simply to the clan but to the tribe. As the
unit enlarged the idea of patriotism expanded. In like
manner patriotism extended from city to state, and finally
to nation. Take Greece, for example. In the early days the
Greek patriot did not care much about Greece, but only
about the particular city in which he lived—Athens, Sparta,
Corinth. So Pericles could say, "Fix your eyes on what
Athens might be and make yourselves her lovers." "He
was," as Winwood Reade puts it, "a good Athenian, but
a bad Greek." Not Greece—but Athens. The same was true
of Italy. Time was when Italy was not a nation but a group
of city-states. The Italian patriot was not nation conscious
but only city conscious: Florence, Naples, Rome, Venice.
Speaking broadly, it was not until the unification of Italy
by the astonishing Garibaldi that love of nation superseded
love of city.

Is not the same thing true of our own country? We began
as thirteen scattered colonies, and the early dwellers in
Rhode Island, Massachusetts, New York, or Virginia, were
much more state conscious than nation conscious. Time
came, however, when we became a nation, and Henry
Clay could say, "I have heard something said about alle-

giance to the South. I know no South, no North, no East, no West, to which I owe any allegiance." This, incidentally, is more than many of us can say today. So the idea of patriotism has expanded, become progressively less restricted and more inclusive: beginning with loyalty to the family, going to loyalty to clan and tribe, city and state, and finally to the nation. And that is where we now are.

Some of us feel, however, that the time has come for patriotism to take another step, maybe its final one. Patriotism must now become global. Perhaps this is what Edith Cavell sensed when she said as she faced the German firing squad during the first World War, "Patriotism is not enough"—not inclusive enough. Love of country to date has been a wall separating us from all others. It must become a door through which we pass to a genuine appreciation of humanity. The old love of country is well represented by the ancient Greek motto: "He who is not a Greek is a barbarian." So spoke the arrogant racialists and nationalists of the long ago. But not so speaks the modern Greek. Over the door of the Gennadeion Library in Athens, given by Americans to the Greek nation, are inscribed these words: "Greeks are they who share life with us." "He who is not a Greek is a barbarian"—that is the old defunct idea of patriotism. "Greeks are they who share life with us"—that is the patriotism that has some future. In other words, we shall have to move from "competitive man" to "co-operative man," from the concept of the "world warrior" to the concept of the "world citizen."

Indeed, we shall have to get over this bugaboo of national sovereignty. Not that we intend to give up our sovereignties, but that somehow we shall have to merge our sovereignties into the greater sovereignty of humanity. Nothing less than this is the price of peace. The idea of sovereignty which sends a nation on the path of unilateral action in complete indifference to the rights of other nations is utterly defunct. It is no longer possible for a nation to do anything it likes, any time it likes, in any way it likes, unless it chooses to imperil the safety of mankind. It is this spirit of so-called national sovereignty which makes our international life archaic, pagan, and uncivilized. Each of us who lives in a civilized community, though free, is by no means sovereign. As individuals we must relinquish much of our "sovereignty." This is the price for living in peace and fellowship with other "sovereign" individuals. In no other way could we civilize community life. So, too, with the state. Each of the states that compose our nation has relinquished some of its sovereign rights. This is the price the state pays for becoming a part of a nation. In no other way could we civilize national life. Similarly, each nation will have to give up some of its sovereignty if it is to become a part of the world's life. This is the price the nation must pay for civilizing international life. In no other way can it be civilized. To insist on complete national sovereignty is to prolong international anarchy and so bring about national disaster, since no nation can be secure in an anarchic world. National sovereignty must go if man is to stay. I like these words of J. B. Priestly. In his novel *Faraway* he makes a character say: "It's not a matter of Englishmen and Frenchmen, . . . it's a matter of men and women. . . . Every time you ignore national boundaries you bring the possibility of a sane, happy, peaceful world

a bit nearer. . . . I'm an Englishman and I love England.
. . . I owe a lot to England. But I owe still more to the
world. . . . You say . . . let's do something for England for
once. But I say, for God's sake, let's do something for civilization for once."

This does not indicate a weakening of our love for our
country. Each man will still love his own country as he
can love no other, just as each man loves his home as he
can love no other. But even as love of home leads to an
appreciation of what is fine and good in all homes, so
should love of country lead to a recognition of what is
good in other countries. The most imperative need before
us now therefore is this transcending of the bigoted barriers of our individual nationalisms and the development
of an international mind. General Dwight D. Eisenhower
said in speaking of the soldier: "He knows that in war
the threat of separate annihilation tends to hold allies
together; he hopes we can find in peace a nobler incentive
to produce the same unity."

It is hard to escape the conclusion that this international
mind which transcends national boundaries is one of the
unique contributions of Christ to mankind. Jesus, as we
have said, loved his country. Yes, but he spoke of the
"other sheep" which were not of this fold, of drawing
"all men" unto himself. "For if ye love them which love
you, what reward have ye?" he asked. Paul referred to
himself as being "of the tribe of Benjamin, an Hebrew of
the Hebrews." But it was Paul who first pushed out beyond
the confines of Judaism and took Christianity to the Gentile world. He was the herald of a kingdom in which
national and racial particularisms would be submerged or

merged into a more inclusive fellowship. There would be neither Greek nor Jew, barbarian, Scythian, bond nor free; but all would be one in a deeper and broader fellowship.

The only kind of war from now on will be global war, and the only way to prevent a global war is by having global concern. Such global concern inheres in the gospel of our God, who has made of one blood all men to dwell upon the face of the earth. We must begin now to live as though that gospel were true. If we can realize now that we are citizens not only of our respective countries but of the world, then perchance these dead shall not have died in vain.

VII

Acquiescence: *The Public*

IN CONSIDERING the evils that were responsible for the crucifixion we cannot omit the part the public may have played. Opinions may differ as to whether the public was to blame at all, and if so, to what extent. From one point of view it would seem as though Jesus was very popular with the public. Several passages of Scripture might be quoted in support of this opinion. "Many were gathered together, insomuch that there was no room to receive them." Again: "He spake to his disciples, that a small ship should wait on him because of the multitude, lest they should throng him." "The multitude cometh together again, so that they could not so much as eat bread." "There were gathered together an innumerable multitude of people, insomuch that they trod one upon another." John relates in connection with the feeding of the five thousand that "when Jesus therefore perceived that they would come and take him by force, to make him a king, he departed again into a mountain himself alone." Not only so, but we are explicitly told that the Sadducean priests "sought how they might kill him; for they feared the people." Such references leave us in no doubt that Jesus was popular with the public. Indeed, even up to his crucifixion, "there followed him a great company of people, and of women, which also bewailed and lamented him."

It might be said, on the other hand, that the public cried, "Crucify him," and, when they might have released

154

him, chose Barabbas. In fairness, however, we must distinguish between the public and the mob that crowded the court and the cross. It was the mob that chose Barabbas, and they were the tool of the priesthood: "The chief priests and elders persuaded the multitude that they should ask Barabbas, and destroy Jesus." The public then must be differentiated from the mob of hirelings and hangers-on who, at the instigation of the priests, demanded his crucifixion. Granting all this, I find it hard to believe that the public was wholly innocent of his death, and that for two reasons.

For one thing, it is difficult to doubt that the public acclaim which the Master received was often based on a misconception and that his popularity waned as his true mission became clearer. The public by and large wanted a leader who would deliver them from Roman rule. Jesus knew this. Not far from the village of Nazareth, about six miles north, was the town of Sepphoris. Here during his boyhood an ill-starred insurrection against Rome was started by one Judas. This was vigorously put down by Varus, a Roman official, who completely destroyed the town in some such way as the Nazis did Lidice. Jesus no doubt saw the flames of Sepphoris from his Nazareth home. They were symbolic of the burning hopes for freedom of his fellow countrymen.

There can be little doubt that at the outset of his ministry the public regarded Jesus as the one who would bring these hopes to fulfillment. They so regarded him even up to the very end, as the Palm Sunday pageant indicates. In no other way can we understand their hosannas. "Blessed is he that cometh in the name of the Lord," they cried.

155

The pathos of that scene, as those who have witnessed the Passion play at Oberammergau will agree, lies in the fact that the popularity of Jesus on that occasion grew out of a misconception. Had the people known the true nature of his kingship, they would not have cheered him as they did. All through Jesus' public ministry, therefore, there was an undercurrent of misunderstanding, of tension, between the expectations of the public and his conception of the ministry which in the providence of God he was called to perform.

If this interpretation is correct, it sheds light on the temptation in the wilderness. The struggle in the soul of Jesus during that experience resulted from his knowledge of what the people wanted and were expecting from him and what he felt was the will of God for him. The first temptation was to turn stones into bread. Was this symbolic of offering the public the physical prosperity which would evoke the gratitude a popular leader would need? Next he was asked to cast himself down from the pinnacle of the temple. Was this one way of drawing a crowd and so enhancing his popularity? Finally he was offered the kingdoms of the world and all the glory of them. This, surely, was a clear appeal to satisfy the hunger for freedom which gnawed at the heart of every loyal Israelite. But this temtation too Jesus resisted. It is evident then that Jesus had no part or lot in the cheap and plausible half-truth "We must give the people what they want." He had bigger business on hand. Peter was only voicing the spirit of his Master when he said, "We ought to obey God rather than men." He would do not what the public wished but what God willed. That was his mission. There seems therefore little reason to doubt that despite the popularity which we have noted, the public, or large sections of it, must have been disappointed in Jesus, since he did not give whole-hearted support to their political and social expectations.

There is another reason why we cannot absolve the public. Why should we believe that the attitude of the public toward the truth in Jesus' day was fundamentally different from the attitude of the public today? Does anyone doubt that in the betrayal and crucifixion of truth today the public is surely to blame? If, therefore, we can discover the attitude of the general public toward the finest and choicest values of our day, we shall not be far from understanding the public's attitude in Jesus' day. Its part, though indirect, was nonetheless decisive. Perhaps we might designate the evils of the public by the word "acquiescence."

It should be said at the outset, however, that in considering the public we are not discussing an entity in which we as Christians have no part. The evils which we may observe in the public are the very ones which in varying degrees dog our own footsteps. Willy-nilly, we, Christian laymen and ministers alike, are a part of the very public whose evils we condemn. The greatest seers and saints, while separated from the world, never regarded themselves as being isolated from it. So Moses said: "Oh, this people have sinned a great sin, and have made them gods of gold. Yet now, if thou wilt forgive their sin—; and if not, blot me, I pray thee, out of thy book." And the Master himself submitted to the rite of baptism, not because he was conscious of any personal guilt, but because he wanted to identify himself with a guilty nation. We must understand, there-

157

fore, that we ourselves, as part of the public, are involved in the very attitudes or evils we deplore. Let us then *in the light of the Cross* consider four major evils which the public sets against the truth—evils which illustrate the acquiescence of the public.

One is ignorance. Jesus encountered this in his day. "He beheld the city, and wept over it, saying, If thou hadst known . . ." There can be little doubt that the public often betrays or crucifies the truth simply because it has never taken the trouble to inform itself of the true nature of the issues at stake. This was just as true in Jesus' day as in ours. His prayer, "Father, forgive them; for they know not what they do," could more often than not be applied to the public, which has a way of remaining quite uninformed on matters of major importance. "For had they known it, they would not have crucified the Lord of glory," wrote Paul.

It is a familiar fact that from the days of the prophets the Bible has tended to identify sin not so much with wickedness as with stupidity. Isaiah represents God as saying, "Israel doth not know, my people doth not consider"; and "Come now, and let us reason together." Another prophet, Hosea, says: "My people are destroyed for lack of knowledge"; and "There is no truth, nor mercy, nor knowledge of God in the land." One remembers, too, Jesus' parable of the wise and foolish builders. We would have said "good" and "bad" where he said "wise" and "foolish." And Jesus said to the people before the empty sepulcher: "O fools, and slow of heart to believe . . ." and of the multitude who followed him to the desert place we read: "And Jesus . . . was moved with compassion toward them, because they were as sheep not having a shepherd." Sheep without a shepherd are always in danger of going astray. They are ready prey for the wily wolf. So is the unthinking public. The loudest voice, the largest advertisement, the brightest light, the currently popular fad, whether in dress or ideas, to these the public turns in pitiful servility. As Henry Sloane Coffin says in *The Meaning of the Cross,* "Behind all earth's tragedies there is a public whose state of mind has much to do with the central event." That "state of mind" is seldom adequately informed. It feeds on the prejudices and half-truths gleaned from newspapers, cheap magazines, radio, and movies, which generally do not aim at the propagation of truth. They are agencies of propaganda. They have their axes to grind. They often capitalize on the most superficial and lowest elements in human nature. They give the public what it wants in order to get from the public what they want—patronage. And so truth is crucified. No wonder the Master was moved with compassion when he saw the multitude. The modern multitude is even in a worse plight, for science has given the modern knave incredible techniques for deceiving and exploiting the unthinking.

Indeed, this evil of being uninformed besets not only the public in general but the church people in particular. Paul, in writing to the Christians of Rome, said: "For I bear them record that they have a zeal of God, but not according to knowledge." Zeal without knowledge, good intentions without accurate and adequate information, have probably been as great a handicap to truth as the evil designs of wicked men. As the old saying puts it,

But evil is wrought by want of thought
As well as want of heart.

To mean well is one thing—to do well, another. Good people need always to remember that good will in the heart was never intended as a substitute for information in the head. It is still sadly true that the children of this world are wiser in their generation than the children of light. The truth about many of our social situations can only be obtained by serious inquiry and patient study. Never mind how much effort may be required, Christians have a God-given duty to be informed. The evil forces of a community often "get away with murder" largely because they can count on the lack of information on the part of good people who simply do not take the trouble to find out what is going on. Evildoers may usually count on a half-awake public. Dr. Coffin in *The Meaning of the Cross* imagines someone busy at his work remarking as the procession moves on to Calvary: "Hello! Another hanging today? Who's to be hung? Those two bandits? Who's the third prisoner? That Prophet from Galilee? Oh, they got Him very quickly, didn't they?" And as the prisoners and Christ file past, the day's work is resumed. "If thou hadst known . . . the things which belong unto thy peace!"

The public acquiesces not only because of ignorance but also because of indifference. There can be little doubt that the Master encountered that evil, too, in his lifetime. We read in Matthew: "He did not many mighty works there because of their unbelief." No doubt some of this unbelief sprang from honest doubt. Much of it, however, then as now, was the result of an indifference to the things of the spirit. In the parable of the sower one wonders whether the wayside soil, so hardened that the truth made no impression, might not be a symbol of the callousness that comes from a complete lack of interest. So, too, in the parable of the marriage feast. We read in the same Gospel: "But they made light of it, and went their ways, one to his farm, another to his merchandise." They were indifferent. At any rate, indifference had its share in erecting the cross. Who can estimate the worthy causes that have perished, the truth that has been crucified, largely because of the deadly indifference of a public that just does not care at all what happens?

There are two sources from which the good is threatened. One is the calculated, aggressive designs of evil men; the other the indifference of the public, among whom incidentally are hosts of good people. In the parable of the tares we are told that it was while the good man slept that the enemy came and sowed tares among the wheat. Sleep then became "the unwitting accomplice of treachery." This I suppose is why the New Testament so often urges watchfulness as a Christian virtue. Good people who are half asleep, not thoroughly aware of what transpires nor concerned about what happens, just indifferent, have been the constant ally of the forces of evil. The shrewd evildoer can usually count on the apathy of an indifferent public. Indeed the problem antidates the time of Christ by several hundred years. It wrung from the heart of Jeremiah, some six hundred years before Christ, one of his most poignant laments: "Is it nothing to you, all ye that pass by?"

One reason why indifference is so deadly a sin is that it never seems deadly. The most dangerous physical diseases

161

are those that give us no evidence of their presence until it is too late to conquer them. Some of the evils we indulge induce violent reactions, as though we had experienced an earthquake shock. They affect us physically, morally, mentally. They plunge us into remorse or regret. They make us exclaim with Peter, "Depart from me; for I am a sinful man, O Lord." But the treacherous aspect of the sin of indifference is that it leaves us wholly undisturbed. It never evokes any violent reaction from us. It creeps up on us like a certain kind of paralysis, extending its deadly poison little by little, until before we know it we are completely infected—and then we do not know it! Such is the nature of this evil that it makes us unconcerned about our unconcern.

Moreover, indifference is a deadly sin not only because it does not seem deadly but also because it is a sin of omission rather than commission, and such sins never seem as bad as those of commission, though often they are very much worse. Robert Louis Stevenson once said, "The only sins worth thinking about are sins of omission." That may seem an exaggeration, yet this statement comes very near to the judgment of Jesus himself. For it is a striking fact that whenever Jesus spoke of hell or eternal damnation he almost invariably connected it with some sin of omission which sprang from indifference. Here for example is the picture of Dives in Hades. What had he done? Nothing! Simply failed to help the poor man at his gate. Or here is the wicked servant cast into outer darkness. What had he done? Nothing—just tied up his talent in a napkin and buried it. Or here are some foolish virgins shut out from the marriage feast. What had they done? Nothing, just neglected to buy oil. Or here is a group of people at the final judgment. They are sent away into eternal darkness. For doing what? For doing nothing—"Inasmuch as ye did it not . . ." In the story of the good Samaritan, what harm did the priest and the Levite do? No positive harm. They just did nothing—passed by on the other side. "Is it nothing to you, all ye that pass by?" One of the greatest condemnations ever passed on a church is pronounced on the church of Laodicea in the book of Revelation. What had it done? Well, it had been neither cold nor hot, neither for nor against—just nauseatingly neutral, lukewarm, indifferent.

One feels almost like saying that the greatest enemy to the cause of Christ today comes not from the aggressive antagonism of evil but from the appalling moral inertia of good. For indifference is a moral frost that chills and kills. Nothing good can possibly grow in the climate it creates. The most baffling part of the matter is that the indifferent are often good people. But they are actually moral parasites that live off the accumulated spiritual resources of a community. From these resources they constantly draw, but, moral misers that they are, they put nothing in the bank. They are "men of the afterglow." They live in the reflected light of those who have gone before. Whatever ideals they possess have been given them by their fathers. But the torch they received will go out in their hands because they are moral and spiritual sluggards who make no effort to keep the torch aglow. These are the people who create the greatest problem for the Christian church. If one had to choose he would rather meet the aggressive enemies of Christianity than these folk who often admit, without argument, that their course is indefensible, but do nothing whatever to change it. No wonder the one class that Dante did not know what to do with in the future world was the indifferent. Neither heaven nor hell wanted them. George Adam Smith put the matter well when he said:

> We have today the same mass of obscure, nameless persons, who oppose their almost unconquerable inertia to every movement of reform, and are the drag upon all vital and progressive religion. The great causes of God and Humanity are not defeated by the hot assaults of the Devil, but by the slow, crushing, glacier-like mass of thousands and thousands of indifferent nobodies. God's causes are never destroyed by being blown up, but by being sat upon. It is not the violent and anarchical whom we have to fear in the war for human progress, but the slow, the staid, the respectable.[1]

A third evil of the public is irresponsibility. Jesus encountered this, too. He told a story once of two men: one who said he would go but did not, the other that he would not but did. "Which of the two did the will of the father?" Jesus asked.[2] It was not the man of large professions and little deeds, who said but did not, and so proved irresponsible. Jesus also told of a would-be follower who enthusiastically said, "Master, I will follow thee whithersoever thou goest." But Jesus dissuaded him. He lacked the character of steadfastness necessary for such an undertaking. In the parable of the unfaithful steward Jesus says: "And that servant, which knew his lord's will, and prepared not himself, neither did according to his will, shall be beaten with many stripes." He continues: "Unto whomsoever much is given, of him shall be much required: and to

[1] Quoted by Walter Russell Bowie, *Which Way Ahead,* p. 49.
[2] Matt. 21:31—Moffatt.

164

whom men have committed much, of him they will ask the more." These and similar statements show that the Master faced the evil of irresponsibility in his day.

That evil is still with us. It still crucifies the truth. For one of the unfailing reactions of the public is that, though quick to blame, it never blames itself. It fails to realize that the very acts it censures are to be laid at its own door. There is an incident in the Gospels which, though it deals with the priesthood, aptly describes this attitude of the public. After Judas had reached that point of disillusionment and remorse which usually follows wrongdoing, he took the thirty pieces of silver back to the chief priests, saying, "I have sinned in that I have betrayed the innocent blood." Judas was seeking some gleam of sympathy and understanding from those who had aided and abetted him in his deed. But it was not to be found. On the contrary the chief priests replied, "What is that to us? see thou to that." Dr. Moffatt's translation reads: "What does that matter to us? it is your affair, not ours!" Although these words were spoken by the priests, they represent one typical reaction of the public. "It is your affair, not ours!" Surely these words are an accurate example of the public's attitude to what happened to Jesus. Jesus was crucified partly by falling through the net of public opinion, which was too loosely woven to catch him or too weakened by apathy and indifference to support him. Many good causes and many good men have died that way, killed by the chilling atmosphere of a public irresponsibility which naïvely says, "What does that matter to us? It is your affair, not ours!"

Of all the ways of losing our sense of personal responsibility, none is so effective as getting into a crowd and acting as part of a group. Perhaps had Judas bargained with *one* priest rather than the priesthood, the reply made to him would have been different. It is much easier to say, "It is your affair, not *ours*," than it is to say, "It is your affair, not *mine*." Indeed, I sometimes think that our sense of personal responsibility diminishes as the size of the group to which we belong, or through which we act, increases. Getting into a group is like getting into an automobile. When two individuals accidentally bump each other on the sidewalk, each is usually full of apologies. If, however, those same individuals get into their respective cars and then bump into each other, they are still full of something—but not usually apologies! Getting into a group, like getting into a car, lowers the sense of personal responsibility. And the bigger the group the smaller the sense of responsibility.

This game of washing our hands of the world's evil is one at which we all play. We take some leader from the underworld who has built up a vast illicit trade of one sort or another and send him to prison. Yet how long could any such man last but for the public who supports his illicit business? We condemn the author of a vulgar book, the producer of a salacious play. Surely they are not innocent. Yet how far could such an author or a producer go without people like you and me who read the book or see the play? A friend of mine says that he went into a store some time ago and asked for a certain article. The clerk said to him: "You are the first man who has asked for that in five years. We used to have a lot of them in stock, but we do not carry them any more. There is no longer a public demand for them." So the demand of the public determines what the stores sell, what the authors

166

write, what the producers put on. How can we say, "It is your affair, not ours"? How far could any Judas get without the co-operation of the priests? What a responsibility rests on us to "covet earnestly the best gifts"!

To most of us Hitler seemed like a Judas. He betrayed the values we hold dear and without which life would be intolerable. Yet it hardly occurred to us that we might in part be responsible for this tyrant. We said in substance to the Germans, "It is your affair, not ours." History will not so regard our role. An impartial study will reveal that those policies followed by the victors at the close of the first World War were largely responsible for the situation that spawned Hitler and his cohorts. Hitler, like Judas, had his priests who aided and abetted him, played into his hands, and among that priesthood stands our own country along with the other victorious democracies. Judas is always helpless without his confederates who, knowingly or otherwise, aid and abet him in his designs. *Our* kiss may not have betrayed the truth, *our* lips may not have pronounced the sentence, *our* hands may not have driven the nails. That, however, does not absolve us. The evildoer is often no more than the focal point at which the infection of the body politic comes to the surface. Humility and repentance then befit the public, not the sort of feigned innocence that springs from a false feeling of irresponsibility.

This evil of irresponsibility besets not only the public in general but also the church in particular. We speak of a revival of religion. By this we usually visualize a movement starting outside among the unchurched and flowing into the church. I venture, however, that the revival most devoutly to be desired is that which would start within the

167

church itself. Too many Protestant Christians are clinkers instead of live coals. They help to smother the flame rather than increase its glow. They "belong" to the church, but the church is no richer for owning them. These are the irresponsible Protestants. Their name is legion. Their names are on the church rolls, and as they are read over it is as though one were reading the death column of a large city newspaper. Such people are usually the most critical and exacting, though they have least reason to be. This is not strange, for there is always a greater spirit of understanding and helpfulness among those who are helping to bear the burden, share the load, play the game, than those who are observing from a distance. The soldier who has been in the heat of battle has a deeper understanding than the one who has never left the parade grounds.

Another aspect of this matter is that to date we have evolved no effective way of bringing the group within the orb of accountability. It is a truism that while we make the individual toe the line, the group often goes scot free. This may be partly due to the fact that not only does the sense of personal responsibility diminish as the size of the group increases but the evil done within the camaraderie of the group never seems so shocking as that done by the individual. History has heaped blame on Judas. His very name has become a synonym of what is treacherous and base. Yet his confederates, the priests, were equally reprehensible. But somehow what *one man* does usually seems worse in our eyes than the deeds of the many. If one man kills he is brought to court as a murderer, but when a mob goes on a lynching spree it is somehow beyond the law. This double standard of morality, one for individuals and the other for groups, is indefensible. We are just now in the process of trying to stop it. That is what the United Nations are attempting. They are saying that nations will no longer be allowed to do as they please but will be held responsible for their actions and judged at the bar of world opinion. For even as making the individual morally accountable was the way of civilizing community life, so making the nation morally responsible will lead to the civilizing of our international life. There is no other way.

Here then are three great evils by which the public in the Master's day, as in ours, crucified the truth: ignorance, indifference, irresponsibility. And there is a fourth, which is perhaps even more baffling, namely, preoccupation. Indeed, Jesus faced this evil even before he knew he faced it. When Joseph and Mary reached Bethlehem they found that there was no room for them in the inn. It was filled. And so he was born in a stable. That incident was symbolic. The plain fact is that Christ and his truth have as much to fear from the innkeepers who may be kindly disposed but overcrowded as from the Herods who would aggressively destroy them.

There are two pertinent illustrations of this truth in the Gospel according to Luke. Jesus said to a certain man: "Follow me. But he said, Lord, suffer me first to go and bury my father. . . . And another also said, Lord, I will follow thee; but let me first go bid them farewell, which are at home at my house." I will follow, but let me first do something else! The second incident is the Master's parable of the great supper: "Come; for all things are now ready. And they all with one consent began to make excuse." One had a pressing business engagement; he had

169

bought a piece of ground and had to go and see it. Another said he had some farm chores; he had bought five yoke of oxen and had to prove them. A third pleaded domestic preoccupations; he had married a wife and so begged to be excused. To this story we might add the graphic parable of the sower, in which Jesus describes the good seed that fell among thorns, which grew up and choked it. Good soil, but so frightfully cluttered up with weeds that there was no room in it for the good seed. It appears then that even in Jesus' day people's minds were so cluttered up and their time so taken up that they had no room for life's greatest values, and those values perished from neglect.

Such very human incidents, narrated by the Master, make it clear that we do have to choose what we shall do and leave undone. We simply do not have time enough nor adequate strength to take on or take in all that the days have to offer. During the war we learned the meaning of priorities. The issues were so great and the times so critical that we had to discipline our desires and use discrimination in our choices. Willy-nilly, we had to put first things first. And so we pushed second-rate matters off stage, behind the wings, and gave precedence to matters of greater moment. The idea behind priorities, however, has always been a valid one, war or no war. Every well-ordered life knows what it means, figuratively speaking, to say "yes" to some comers and "no" to others, to close the door to some visitors and open it to others, to let some customers stand in line and wait while others are served first. It was Ruskin who asked us to remember that if we read this, we cannot read that. His observation is true not of reading only but of life in general. Our preoccupation with the second-rate has sealed the fate of many first-rate values. Jesus was crucified because the public by and large were just too busy to be bothered about what happened to him.

Now one of the strange paradoxes of life is that one finds room so much more easily for the worthless than for the worth-while. Nothing is quite so easy as to fill one's life so full of the second-rate that the choicest values cannot even gain standing room. The indifference of large sections of the public to the gospel is not rooted in any positive hostility or aggressive ill will, but is due to the fact that there is literally no room in the inn. Whenever life is overcrowded, it is usually the best that is crowded out. There are at least two reasons for this. One is that the bad is more in evidence. There are more weeds than flowers and, what is more, you do not have to cultivate weeds. All one has to do to get his garden to grow a crop of weeds is just to do nothing. And that is all we need to do to fill our life with the tawdry—just open the gate or let down the bars and allow nature to take its course. The Master said the kingdom of heaven was like a man *seeking* goodly pearls —"Seek, and ye shall find." It takes effort to find pearls. They are beautiful and rare. If it is junk we are after the quest need not take us beyond the attic or the basement.

There is, however, another reason for our preoccupation with the second-rate or the positively bad—namely, that evil dramatizes itself as the good never does. "Satan himself is transformed into an angel of light," observed Paul. Evil therefore has a way of arresting our attention as the good does not. "Asses bray but gentlemen speak low." There is profound truth in the statement of Jesus that

171

"the devil . . . is a liar." This means that there is an element of deception in all evil. Sin never presents itself as it really is. If it did we should not, I suppose, "fall for it" so readily. It may be this element in evil that has caused the seers to identify the wicked with the stupid. Were we wise enough to see through the façade of evil to its real nature, we should avoid it. One wonders, for example, how many immature young people and immature adults have fallen into the drink habit, lured by all the glamour and social éclat which astute advertising has placed about that damnable industry. There are enough lies told in liquor advertising in our country in one day to make Ananias blush.

Consider this liquor question a little more in detail. Is it because we love to believe lies and take delight in being deceived that this traffic has gained such a strangle hold on the American public? According to figures released by the United States Department of Commerce, during the year 1945 we spent for liquor in this country of ours more than $7,700,000,000, an increase of $700,000,-000 over the year 1944. The sum is so staggering that it really means nothing. Perhaps a few comparisons might help make it real. In the school year 1941-42 the total expenditure in the United States for education—meaning for public and private schools, all elementary and secondary schools, all colleges and universities and professional schools, teachers' colleges and normal schools, schools for delinquents, the blind, deaf, and mentally deficient, federal schools for Indians—amounted to slightly over $3,000,-000,000. Our total expenditure for 6,000 public libraries,

1,600 college and university libraries, 28,000 public school libraries, was for the same year slightly over $86,000,000.[3] Our national expenditure for gifts and bequests to organized religion in 1942, according to *Survey of Business,* June, 1944, was $720,800,000. So in this country of ours we spend more than twice as much on liquor as we do on education, and more than ten times as much as we do on organized religion. When Paul wrote of those "whose God is their belly," he wrote more truly than he knew. This god is winning an increasing number of devotees as the years go by.

What has this nation of ours to show for the $7,700,000,-000 a year that we spend for liquor? It is impossible to tabulate the deterioration of our physical and moral fiber through the excessive use of alcohol. (Too much praise cannot be given to the singular work of Alcoholics Anonymous in reclaiming individuals whose lives have been thus affected.) Three results, however, are plain enough to have received public attention: an alarming increase in automobile accidents, often fatal; in broken homes; and in juvenile delinquency (which is due primarily to adult delinquency)—to each of which liquor is without the slightest doubt a major contributing factor. Prohibition may not have been the answer. But anyone who thinks that what we now have is the answer would do well to have his mind examined.

There is yet another reason why we allow the bad to crowd out the good. It is because it is so much easier to act on the policy "first come, first served" than to discrimi-

[3] Report of U. S. Office of Education, 1941-42.

nate. There is a streak, if not a sizable chunk, of moral laziness in all of us. Our moral inertia is a millstone about our necks. To choose the good often necessitates a deliberate act of will which runs counter to our inclinations. "Strait is the gate . . . which leadeth unto life." The lure of the broad way is that it is effortless. We avoid the morally strenuous. The fact that we do reveals our ignorance or immaturity, or both. Left to themselves, few children would ever go to school. In youth our choice of the easy way is overruled by the authority of our elders. Such authority ceases as we mature. But physical maturity never of itself insures moral competence. We sometimes say to an adult, "Why don't you act your age?" And rightly, for often adults manifest all the peevishness, sulkiness, and insolence of a spoiled child.

The danger of preoccupation would not be so great if the choice before us were always between the bad and the good, the worthless and the worth-while. Such, however, is not the case. It is often a choice not between the bad and the good but between the good and the better, the better and the best. This is clearly evident as we examine the incidents in the Gospels which we have already noted. The matters which the men in Jesus' parables were busy about were not of themselves bad or worthless. One had to go to a funeral, another had some home duties to attend to, still another had a business engagement, and so on. You could not send a man to jail for attending to any of these matters, nor in the doing of them would he be engaged in anything dishonorable or base. One fancies that the Master deliberately chose these incidents to show how the good may become the enemy of the better. The occu-

174

pations about which Martha was careful and troubled were not wicked or base. They were good, but Mary had chosen "the better part." Herein lies the most difficult choices a man ever has to make. Our problem is not simply to keep the bad from crowding out the good, but also to keep the good from becoming an enemy of the better and the best. There is no reason to suppose that the Bethlehem inn was full of gangsters, murderers, or crooks. Its register would have revealed the names of good, respectable people. But Christ was crowded out just the same. Even so is he crowded out of our lives.

And so the public, through ignorance, indifference, irresponsibility, and preoccupation, acquiesced in the crucifixion of Jesus. Through the same evils the truth still suffers at its hands. It has not been possible to make the public's role as clear and definite as that of the other evils discussed, for they were associated with specific individuals or groups. In the nature of the case, the public's part would be more general; yet there can be little doubt that the public created the climate or set the stage for the drama of the crucifixion. What is the answer to these evils of the public? The answer is found, not in the public, but in the individuals like you and me who compose it. Although we have been dealing with some of the social problems or evils of Jesus' day, as of ours, we must not forget that, while snatching brands from the burning is not an adequate method of eliminating our social evils, the individual is still the key to the social situation.

We may learn from the Master in this matter. He was moved with compassion when he saw the multitude, and he preached to them; but his primary concern was not

175

with the multitude. His significant work was done with
individuals. It was through individuals that he sought to
change the multitude and the world. "When a society is
hopelessly corrupt and incapable of reforming its institutions," says Lewis Mumford in *The Condition of Man,*
"it is the individual who must first be saved."

This was the emphasis of Jesus. In dealing with individuals he did not try to snatch them out of a doomed society as brands from the burning. Rather he redeemed
them within the framework of their social relationships
and so made them redeemers through the power of his
spirit. It was through changing individuals in this manner
that he sought to change society. As we read the New
Testament we are amazed at the number and variety of
the individuals with whom Jesus dealt. They come walking out at us from its pages: Peter, Matthew, Philip, Nicodemus, Zacchaeus, the rich young ruler, Mary, Martha,
Lazarus, the Roman centurion—to mention a few. If Nicodemus could be born again and Zacchaeus be made honest,
if Thomas could become a man of faith and Peter be made
steadfast, then these individuals, like the leaven or the
salt, could influence the group. For, as Mr. Mumford says,
"once a change is effected in the person, every group will
record and respond to it."

It is inevitable, I suppose, that we should evaluate the
significance of movements or organizations by quantitative
tests. Yet it is always well to remember that the hope of
the many lies in the few, perhaps in the one. The best
proof of this is found in the very Man in the light of whose
cross we have been considering the sins of mankind. That
"one solitary life" has changed the course of history—

changed it by changing individuals. Through transformed individuals he has been changing the world ever since— "the true Light, which lighteth every man that cometh into the world"—and because he enlightens every man he will yet illumine the world: Jesus Christ, Son of God, Saviour.

VIII

Salvation: *The Christ*

WE HAVE BEEN studying the evils that were responsible
for the crucifixion of the Master. We have watched them
close in on him until they finally cornered, captured, and
crucified him. It was a true insight that led the synoptic
writers to record that as Jesus died "there was darkness
over the whole land." Truly, that was one of the very
darkest moments in human history. For the death of Jesus
was more than the death of a man. With him died too the
faith, vision, and values that he preached and lived. On
Good Friday evening, if ever, Truth was on the scaffold
and Wrong on the throne. The forces of evil strutted off
with their flags flying while Truth, worsted in the encoun-
ter, lay bleeding. It seemed indeed as though man had won
the victory over God.

To no people did that victory seem more certain and
final than to his disciples. Although they may never fully
have comprehended the message and mission of Jesus, and
certainly were often perplexed at his methods—which, as
we have seen, bore little resemblance to those which tradition had taught them to expect of the Messiah—still
they trusted him implicitly and may have hoped to the
last that somehow he would be delivered from the hand
of his enemies.

Any such hope, however, was now quite dead, as dead as
their beloved leader seemed when his lifeless body was
laid in Joseph's tomb. The darkness that covered the land

was hardly as deep as that which enshrouded the disciples' minds and hearts. In but a little while they had fallen from the heights of expectation to the depths of despair. It was now their task, as S. Pearce Carey has said, "to build their life as realists upon a shrunken scale amid the debris of their dreams." And, realists that they were, they began to do just that. To their tasks they would return: "Simon Peter saith unto them, I go a fishing. They say unto him, We also go with thee." Presently, however, an event transpired that transformed their lives and so changed the course of human history—the resurrection of Jesus from the dead.

It is not my purpose to discuss the resurrection in detail except to say that in a certain sense it may be regarded as the best-attested fact of history. To be sure, there are differences, if not discrepancies, in the resurrection narratives as given in the Gospels. Not only are there differences in the Gospel narratives, but there is a difference between the Gospels and the account as given by Paul. His is the earliest record of the resurrection in the New Testament. In it he says nothing about the physical body or the empty tomb, upon which the Gospels lay much stress. Paul, who probably never saw the Master in the flesh, spiritualizes his concept of the resurrection. This may have been because Paul, though heir to the Hebrew tradition, was influenced by his Greek training. The Greeks thought of the future life in terms not of the resurrection of the body but of the immortality of the soul. Their concept of the future life was less material and more spiritual than that of the Hebrews. Paul therefore uses a phrase to describe the risen Christ which shows both his Hebrew and Greek influence. He speaks of a "spiritual body." The phrase is

179

unique with him and comes, I suppose, as near as possible to putting into words a truth which will always be beyond the reach of our earthly experience, and so can never be adequately described.

The form of the resurrection, however, does not concern us now, but the fact of it does, and it is difficult to see how we could doubt the fact. "Belief in the resurrection of Jesus is the motive power of all Christian mankind," says Dmitri Merezhkovski in *Jesus Manifest*. "From what did this faith spring? From five or six remarkably vivid hallucinations? To think so is just as absurd as to suppose that five or six sparks would make water boil in a huge cauldron." There are many historic events that cannot be explained apart from the resurrection. The church is one; but for the resurrection there would be no church. Such pictures as are given in the opening chapters of the book of Acts would be inexplicable and incredible on any other assumption than that Jesus had conquered death. The Christian church is not a monument to a fallen hero but a witness to a living Lord. That is the foundation upon which the church rests.

Nor can we, apart from the resurrection, explain the early preaching. Peter's sermon at Pentecost is typical of all the early preaching: "Ye men of Israel, hear these words; Jesus of Nazareth, a man approved of God among you, . . . ye have taken, and by wicked hands have crucified and slain: whom God hath raised up, having loosed the pains of death: because it was not possible that he should be holden of it." [1]

[1] Acts 2:22-24.

180

Moreover, without the resurrection there would be no gospel, certainly no gospel of salvation. "Behold the Lamb of God, which taketh away the sin of the world." "Thou shalt call his name Jesus: for he shall save his people from their sins." "For the Son of man is come to seek and to save that which was lost." "For unto you is born this day in the city of David a Saviour, which is Christ the Lord." [2] The gospel is good news, and the heart of the good news is that God in Christ has won the victory over sin and death and so stands ready to offer man salvation from these two great enemies of his progress. "I am not ashamed of the gospel of Christ: for it is the power of God unto salvation to every one that believeth." [3] Such words would be meaningless apart from the resurrection. Salvation is the fruit of the resurrection. To speak of a Christ whose life ended in a cemetery as being the Saviour of mankind would be absurd. The fitting symbol for such a life would be the epitaph "Here lies . . ." Christ is the one exception to that rule; his epitaph reads: "He is not here: for he is risen." "But now is Christ risen from the dead, and become the firstfruits of them that slept. . . . For as in Adam all die, even so in Christ shall all be made alive." A living Christ, a triumphant Christ, and therefore a Christ who saves!

In thinking of Christ as our Saviour, we must first realize that obviously we need a Saviour. The plight of man, especially now, is so desperate that even the most self-assured humanist must begin to see the truth in the prophet Jeremiah's words: "O Lord, I know that the way of man

[2] John 1:29; Matt. 1:21; Luke 19:10; 2:11.
[3] Rom. 1:16.

is not in himself; it is not in man that walketh to direct his steps." The same prophet spoke to his people these words which have such a strangely modern ring: "For my people have committed two evils; they have forsaken me the fountain of living waters, and hewed them out cisterns, broken cisterns, that can hold no water." Consider just two of the broken cisterns. Men have sought salvation in power. So the Messiah of the Jews of old was visualized as a warrior king. In like manner men have sought salvation through power even until now. Despite the disillusionments of two world wars in one generation, power is still the divinity that occupies the throne in Moscow, London, Washington, and Paris. But power, whether it be political, economic, or military, is a broken cistern. Power will never save mankind, for man cannot be trusted with power. Lord Acton's familiar dictum still stands: "Power tends to corrupt, and absolute power corrupts absolutely."

> ... O, it is excellent
> To have a giant's strength, but it is tyrannous
> To use it like a giant.

But that is how the giant invariably uses it. For power puts the emphasis on might, not right; and when might vanquishes right we are not saved but deceived; we do not find the way out but are more deeply lost. Power may be useful in the hands of a "saved" man, but power will not save man. "Not by might, nor by power, but by my spirit, saith the Lord of hosts."

So, too, men have regarded knowledge as their savior, and have assumed that as knowledge advanced, the evils that plague mankind would progressively disappear even as darkness before dawn. This assumption presupposes that the primary trouble with man is in his mind and hence that the cure is the light of knowledge. But this is not so. Ignorance is indeed an enemy of man, but it is by no means the most formidable, nor does it hold the key position in the line. The key to the human problem lies not in man's mind but in his will. This is why the Christian diagnosis of the human situation has nothing of the superficiality of the secular diagnosis, which naïvely identifies progress in knowledge with progress. Paul said long ago: "For I delight in the law of God after the inward man: but I see another law in my members, warring against the law of my mind, and bringing me into captivity to the law of sin which is in my members. O wretched man that I am! who shall deliver me from the body of this death? I thank God through Jesus Christ our Lord." [4]

That deeper area of reality which such searching words uncover is one that our secularized education does not come within gunshot of reaching. The strengthening of the will, the disciplining of the emotions, whence our actions usually spring, are outside the pale of our secularized education. That is why knowledge of itself, instead of being our salvation, bids fair to be the main agent in our destruction. In truth, the advance of secular knowledge, instead of removing the evils that threaten to destroy, has only shown those evils in bolder relief. Instead of solving the problem it has made it more acute. For we now see that in no small measure modern man's predicament springs from the fact that intellectually he is a giant while morally and spiritually he is a pigmy. He has devised scientific

[4] Rom. 7:22-25.

techniques which he has not the moral and spiritual maturity to control. He stands at a fork in the road and at this moment does not know whether survival or destruction is to be his lot. No! secularized knowledge has not and never can save us. It has only made more clear and imperative our need of a Saviour.

Granted, however, man's need for salvation, the claim that Christ can meet that need may seem an astonishing one. On the face of it, to go back to the first century in search of a savior for today seems a most unpromising undertaking. Is it not as if a modern architect who wants to build a skyscraper should go back to Bethlehem and consult the man who built the manger? Or as if some modern captain of industry, harassed by the highly complicated economic problems of our age, should consult the employer of the shepherds who kept watch over their flocks by night? It would seem that we have moved so far away from first-century Palestine that to go back there to find a savior may seem to some moderns well-nigh naïve.

But now how far actually have we moved? You know we live in two worlds—one the world out there, the other the world in here; one the world of things, the other the world of thoughts, motives, purposes. The world "out there" has changed incredibly since Jesus was born. I have been thinking of what might happen could we bring back George Washington and set him down in the White House. Poor George Washington, how nonplused he would be! If you asked him whether he would care to go for a ride in an automobile, he would not know what you were talking about. If you told him he was wanted on the phone he would not know a telephone from an iceless refrigerator. If you asked him whether he would like to sit before the radio on Christmas Day and listen to a speech by his "namesake," George VI of Great Britain, then he would think that America had become a land of spooks or fairies. Any six-year-old boy, in matters "out there," could make the father of his country seem like a numskull. The world "out there" has changed incredibly in two hundred years.

But were you to ask George Washington about moral values, whether he thought it was better to be honest than to be dishonest, pure than impure, he would "get" you. Were you to talk with him about the lure of beauty, the appeal of goodness, the quest of truth, he would understand every word you say and could probably give you some pointers. Washington, the city, has been radically changed, but not so Washington, the man. As a matter of fact, do we not take far too seriously these gadgets of modern civilization? It is well for us to remember that because we give our plays in air-conditioned theaters it does not follow that we write better plays than Shakespeare. The fact that the old broom made of twigs has been replaced by the vacuum cleaner has not prolonged the marriage contract, any more than has the electric dishwater protected the youth of our homes from the perils of our secularized society. The fact that we can travel four hundred miles an hour has not made us any more sure of our direction. To be in a tremendous haste to get nowhere is not a significant undertaking. There is a world "out there" of constant flux, novelty, and change. There is a world "in here" of thought, motive, insight, and purpose, which remains surprisingly constant despite the novelties of our civilization. George Buttrick put the matter well when he wrote, in *The Christian Fact and Modern Doubt*: "The automobile has not moved the bases of right and wrong, or of love and hate. . . . To misrepresent a secondhand automobile is essentially no different from misrepresenting an old horse. . . . Human nature is human nature still despite the radio. Perhaps it is all the more human: heretofore we had music, whereas now we have advertising with incidental music." To think then that Jesus has no message for us because, whereas he walked, we fly; whereas he used a rowboat, we use a luxury liner, would be like saying that Paul's great letter on love means nothing since Paul never used a dictaphone, or that Lincoln's Gettysburg Address is unimportant because he did not have it typed.

If then man needs salvation, and if modern man is fundamentally no different from the men of Jesus' day to whom he brought new life, we are prepared now to discuss somewhat more in detail what we mean when we speak of Jesus as our Saviour.

Of course we should emphatically realize that it would be foolish to allow our preoccupation with *how* God in Christ transforms human life to obscure the fact that he *does*. "If any man be in Christ, he is a new creature." So wrote Paul, speaking out of his own experience. How well he knew that! However one may explain what happened to Saul of Tarsus on the Damascus Road, it is certain something did happen which made him a different person. That Damascus Road on which a man is brought face to face with Christ and so becomes a different man— that road runs all through history and is to be found in every country. Christ has been meeting men on that road every day in every age, and in varying degrees making different men of them. That Jesus has been changing the lives of men and women of every age and clime down through the centuries until now is a fact as validly established as any fact historic or scientific could conceivably be.

In trying to understand and explain this fact our fathers used words which unfortunately do not mean too much to many moderns: atonement, regeneration, redemption, reconciliation, justification, sanctification, salvation. Upon these historic words, rich in their theological implications, the great Christian thinkers of all ages have brooded long and deeply. To make such words, every one of which contains an eternal truth, as meaningful to Christians today as they were to our fathers is a task that needs to be done, and must be done if Christianity is to remain true to its historic heritage. Our concern just now, however, is with the ethical rather than the theological implications of salvation, if it be possible to separate them. Let us then *in the light of the Cross* see what we mean when we speak of Jesus as the Saviour of man—first, of individual man. Peter's words provide a good approach: "His name through faith in his name hath made this man strong, whom ye see and know."

We begin with a name, and a name suggests a person. So when we speak of Jesus as Saviour we are thinking first of all, not of doctrine or dogma, but of a person. Christ, not Christianity, is the starting point. Salvation in a personal sense means first of all coming to know Christ—personal-

187

ly. Christ saves the man who comes to know him. Francis Palgrave wrote:

> Dim tracts of time divide
> Those golden days from me;
> Thy voice comes strange o'er years of change;
> How can we follow thee?
>
> Comes faint and far thy voice
> From vales of Galilee;
> Thy vision fades in ancient shades;
> How should we follow thee?

But Robert Browning comes nearer the truth when he says:

> To me, that story—ay, that Life and Death
> Of which I wrote "it was"—to me, it is;
> —Is, here and now. . . .

It is no exaggeration to say that Christ is more real to millions of individuals in this world today than many of their contemporaries are. Paul voiced the truth once for all in his oft-repeated words: "I live; yet not I, but Christ liveth in me: and the life which I now live in the flesh I live by the faith of the Son of God, who loved me, and gave himself for me."

Now when one comes to know Christ as a person there is one fact of which he becomes very conscious, namely that Christ has great faith in his spiritual possibilities. He said to two fishermen, "Follow me, and I will make you fishers of men." Jesus changed men by making them believe that they could become different people from what they were. He had unbounded faith in man. He saw the dark side of human nature, but it was never so dark as to hide the glorious possibilities of each human soul. Even as a great sculptor sees in the crudest block of marble a statue of fine and noble proportions, so Christ in the most unpromising life saw great promise. His emphasis was unlike much of modern Protestant theology, which confronts us, as Canon Raven suggests, with "an inverted Pharisaism that prides itself on its own damnation, exalts Satan as lord of the earth, and thanks God for the good news of original sin." On the contrary, Jesus

> Saw into the depths of human souls,
> Souls that appear to have no depth at all
> To careless eyes.[5]

Knowing ourselves as we do, we should despair of ourselves were it not for the fact that the Master never despairs of us, even at our worst. "For scarcely for a righteous man will one die: yet peradventure for a good man some would even dare to die. But God commendeth his love toward us, in that, while we were yet sinners, Christ died for us." [6] Jesus was realistic in dealing with people. He knew what was in man, knew the very worst about him, yet despite this believed the best about him. His attitude toward his fellows was positive, not negative. One who comes to know Jesus comes to realize that Jesus has more faith in him than he has in himself, sees possibilities in him of which he is unaware, and by this faith helps him to become what otherwise he could not be. "As many as re-

[5] Quoted from James Moffatt, *Love in the New Testament*, p. 209.
[6] Rom. 5:7-8.

189

ceived him, to them gave he power to become the sons of God." [7]

Let us consider this faith as it expressed itself in three different ways. For one thing Jesus believed that people, even the worst people, had the capacity to apprehend spiritual truth. Passing one day through Samaria, that forbidden country to the orthodox Jew, he met a woman at a well. Consider that woman. From the story we are led to believe that she had no culture, no education, no refinement—certainly no morals. We should describe her as a bad character. Yet think of what Jesus said to this uncouth outcast. He gave her some of the most spiritual of his religious concepts. He spoke to her of the water of life that could spring up within her unto everlasting life. It was to her he said, "God is a Spirit"—something which he had not said even to his disciples. We are tempted to save our finest utterances and our ablest thought for our largest and most cultured audience. What an example is this of Jesus giving his best to one human life at its worst! This indicates his profound faith in people. He believed that even the worst can apprehend spiritual truth. He believed there was a chamber in this woman's heart for God if only he could discover the right key, that there was a chord in her nature that could be set in sympathetic vibration if only he could strike the right note, that there was a live coal in her being that could be coaxed into a flame if only the air could reach it. The woman vindicated his faith, and history has vindicated it time and time again, as the missionary enterprise overwhelmingly proves.

[7] John 1:12.

190

But he went further than that. Not only did he believe in the capacity of ordinary human beings to apprehend the truth; he believed further that his truth when apprehended could radically change human nature. This was the point of his conversation with Nicodemus. The difference between Nicodemus and the woman at the well is a striking one. They stood at opposite extremes. She was a peasant, he an aristocrat. She was poor and he one of the wealthiest men in all Jewry. She was an outcast of a despised race, he one of the most respected and respectable men of his day. She had no background of culture or refinement, he was "the teacher of Israel" (A. S. V.). And to this man Jesus said, "Ye must be born again." In other words, "Your nature can and must be changed." "How can these things be?" asked Nicodemus—which shows that his problem, unlike that of the woman, was not moral but intellectual. He apparently apprehended the truth in Jesus. He said, "Rabbi, we know that thou art a teacher come from God." But he did not see how this truth could change one's life.

Nicodemus has had many successors through the years, but I should think that the Nicodemuses of today should at last have been brought to realize that nothing on earth is so easily changed as human behavior. We have seen it happen before our eyes. A man called Adolf Hitler got the youth of Germany to fall in love with him—not only youth but adults too. He said to his people, "Follow me," and they followed him. He became *der Führer*. Under the power of his magnetism he converted a nation that has given to the world some of her greatest musicians, scientists, theologians, and philosophers into a group of raving fanatics. While the sophisticated Nicodemuses were ask-

191

ing, "How can these things be?" Mr. Hitler was showing us that they could be. There is no question about changing human behavior—the only question is whether it will be changed for the better or the worse. We have seen it on a wholesale scale changed for the worse. Christ changes it for the better. Every Christian knows that. It is not theory but fact, irrefutable fact—"from darkness to light, and from the power of Satan unto God."

But Christ took still another step. Not only did he believe that human beings could apprehend the truth and that truth when apprehended could change human nature, but he believed further that human nature when changed could become creative. He said to his disciples: "He that believeth on me, the works that I do shall he do also; and greater works than these shall he do."

There are three main ways in which human personality finds expression: the destructive, the possessive, the creative. In war we are first of all destructive; in peace we tend to be first of all possessive; in Christ we may become creative. The Promised Land of the Old Testament was a material entity to be possessed. The Promised Land of the New Testament is a spiritual ideal, the kingdom of God, to be created by sharing God's redemptive purpose. It is perhaps fair to say that by and large the Old Testament tends to be more materialistic in its concepts than the New. So salvation in the Old Testament was conceived first of all as material deliverance from Egyptian bondage or Babylonian captivity. Later, however, men began to perceive that outward calamities were often the result of inward alienation from God or rebellion against his righteous will. In the New Testament this idea is central. In Revelation

192

we read, "Behold, I make all things new." Christ calls us
not to possess the world that is but, by partaking of his
life-giving spirit, to create the world that ought to be.

The disciples did not at first realize this. They were wont
to think of the rewards of Christian fellowship primarily
in material terms, as when Peter said that they had left all
and followed him, and asked what they would receive.
"Your reward shall be great, and ye shall be the children of
the Highest," Jesus once told them. They thought they
were going to get something; the Master said they would
become something—"children of the Highest." They
would share in God's creative purpose. The disciples, like
their Master, became the spiritual pioneers of their generation—trail blazers on the path to the abundant life. We
think then of Christ as the Saviour of the individual because of his great faith in us: the faith that we can apprehend spiritual truth, that truth when apprehended will
change our nature, that our natures when changed will become capable of endless creative living—"endless" because
death will not destroy those personalities who have shared
God's redemptive purpose and known his love.

But now let us think of Jesus as Saviour not only of the
individual but of the world. We sometimes speak about
the "personal" as opposed to the "social" gospel. Jesus
never made that distinction. Sometimes as one reads the
Gospels, catches the sweep of Christ's vision and the out-
reach of his spirit, it seems as though the Master were
speaking through a gigantic loud-speaker so that the whole
world might hear him. Then again one feels as though
Christ were at one end of a telephone carrying on a conversation over a private wire with just one human being.

"To all nations," he said, and "to every creature." How wise the Master was in this dual emphasis! Every human life is a bundle of relationships that reach far and wide; it is those relationships that make the individual a person. There is therefore no way of saving a person apart from his world, as though he lived in a vacuum. It is inevitable then that we should think of Jesus as the Saviour not only of the individual but of the world—"God so loved the world . . ." We think of Jesus as the Saviour of the world because he has posited new social objectives for men—objectives which if taken seriously would change every major relationship of human life and so would save the world.

There is this difference between a leader and a savior: A leader is one who accepts the current goals or behavior patterns of his age and leads his people on to a realization of them. A savior is one who questions the validity of the objectives themselves and, should he find them self-defeating or vain, projects new ones. A dictator leads his people, but, contrary to the hopes he arouses, he is not their savior; he is their destroyer, because he leads them to self-defeating ends—a fact which all his arrogant bellowing does not change. But not only a dictator does this. The great dangers that imperil human life today come from the fact that our aims are wrong, our objectives are inadequate. Consider some of these aims.

Take wealth. Jesus came into a world in which men thought that the primary values of life were material. He would not accept that goal. Unquestionably he believed in the importance of material things. Much of his ministry was spent meeting the physical, material needs of mankind. When the Master met someone his first thought was not, "I must proceed at once to save his soul." Rather he first of all met his physical need. So he fed the hungry, healed the sick, helped the helpless. The body was the temple of God, and its legitimate material needs were not overlooked even by the most spiritual-minded man who has ever lived. Indeed, so important did he regard the physical, material needs of mankind that the only man with whom he ever identified himself was the man in need. He said that when we help a man in need we are really helping him: "Inasmuch as ye have done it unto one of the least of these my brethren, ye have done it unto me." But Jesus never regarded material values as ends—they were means to an end. He never identified life with them. The habit of equating the worth of a man with the amount of money he possesses would be regarded by him as blasphemy—"The life is more than meat." He said: "Man shall not live by bread alone, but by every word that proceedeth out of the mouth of God."

In the world into which Jesus came, however, the material was regarded as the *summum bonum*. Wealth then as now was popularly accepted as the pearl of great price. He saw men putting money before their own soul's salvation. He told a story about a rich man who prospered and so pulled down his barns and built greater. The fault of this man was not that he prospered—which may have been an indication of his industry, ability, or thrift, none of which Christ would have condemned—but rather that his increased prosperity made him a materialist who was so completely befuddled that he even thought he could feed his soul on things: "Soul, thou hast much goods laid up for many years; take thine ease." Jesus called this man a fool, and reminded him of how pitifully inadequate his wealth would appear when his soul should stand naked before God: "This night thy soul shall be required of thee: then whose shall those things be, which thou hast provided?" He saw men allowing money to make them so selfish as to kill the spirit of sympathy and compassion. In short, he saw that the pursuit of material ends could become so preoccupying and engrossing that a man would not only neglect himself and his neighbor but lose completely his capacity to appreciate or appropriate the eternal values of goodness, truth, and beauty; so much so that it would actually be easier for a camel to go through the eye of a needle than for such a man to enter the kingdom of heaven—the kingdom of the mind and of the spirit. Jesus then has put before us a new goal. Money is not the first thing; business is not the first thing. Man is not an economic animal but a spiritual being. "Seek ye first the kingdom of God, and his righteousness; and all these things shall be added unto you." What a vast change in human relationships would be wrought, from how many evils would we be saved, could we but take this goal seriously!

Another of the self-defeating ideas Jesus refused to accept was that of race superiority. Somebody asked an old rabbi why God made only two people, Adam and Eve. He replied, "So that nobody can say, 'I come from better stock than you do.'" But the people of Jesus' day had forgotten that. Not only of his day but of ours, too. Mr. Hitler may have thought he was being very original in his utterly stupid and wholly unscientific gospel of racial superiority. He was, of course, being painfully old-fashioned. Jesus came into a world filled with racial bitterness. Greeks, Romans, and Jews all peered at each other from behind walls of snobbery and prejudice, each group regarding itself as the racially elite. But Jesus would not be walled in. Walls always shut out more than they shut in. The God whom Jesus came to reveal could not be kept behind these walls built by human pride or human prejudice. Jesus therefore would not stay behind such barriers. He gave mankind a new concept—not racial arrogance but brotherhood.

Up to the time that Jesus came the relationship between man and man had been that of master and slave, or superior and inferior. Men had missed the most significant of all relationships, namely, the relationship of brothers. That was the relationship that Jesus came to reveal. He would not accept the unscientific and cruel racial patterns of his generation. He saw the human race as a family, since God is our father and "hath made of one blood all nations of men . . . to dwell on all the face of the earth." "Behold my mother and my brethren! . . . whosoever shall do the will of my Father . . . is my brother." How long would all our bigoted attitudes last if we could remember that? These areas of our relationships, racial or international, are like a powder keg today—full of explosive material. The wind is stirring in the mulberry trees. Races are getting nearer, not only because of the physical proximity due to the shrinking of our planet as science increasingly knits the nations together, but also because of the widespread awakening of the racially and economically underprivileged to their inherent rights. So the problem before us now is, will the result be conflict or co-operation, helpfulness or hatred? Will we learn to live together, or face the possi-

197

bility of not living at all? The answer depends upon whether we are willing to accept Christ's proffered goal of brotherhood. That would change our relationships. When we think of race, whose attitude do we accept, Hitler's or Christ's?

Another objective with which Jesus would have nothing to do was power. We have already noted the inadequacy of power. The world into which Jesus came recognized by and large only one sort of power—physical power, brute power—and only one expression of power—domination and overlordship. This does not mean that there was no kindness in Jesus' world, but it does mean that it was a foregone conclusion that the strong should lord it over the weak. What else could they do with their strength? So Rome, the proud mistress of the world, ruled with her powerful legions. Shakespeare not unjustly describes this power as he writes of Julius Caesar:

> Why, man, he doth bestride the narrow world
> Like a Colossus; and we petty men
> Walk under his huge legs, and peep about
> To find ourselves dishonourable graves.

This concept of power has had its devotees from the days of the Caesars until now. It has been glorified by Nietzsche with his gospel of the superman. Once at Frankfurt, as he saw a troop of cavalry pass, there came a perception out of which grew his entire philosophy. "I felt for the first time," he said, "that the strongest and highest Will to Life does not find expression in a miserable struggle for existence, but in a Will to War, a Will to Power, a Will to Overpower!" Power was Nietzsche's god, and that the power of a tyrant. Said he, "The dream is dispelled which made the State begin with a contract. What has he to do with contracts who can command, who is master by nature, who comes on the scene with violence in deed and demeanour?" Consequently he hated all thought of democracy—"this mania for counting noses," as he called it. He continued: "Shop-keepers, Christians, cows, women, Englishmen, and other democrats belong together." "Man shall be educated for war, and woman for the recreation of the warrior; everything else is folly."[8]

This philosophy of force and tyranny unashamed has had sickening expression in the exploits of Adolf Hitler. He lived it out. He tried and came very near succeeding in bestriding the narrow world like a Colossus. Hitler and his empire are gone to dust, but the idea that produced them is unfortunately not yet dead. You have only to mark the attitude of the victor to the vanquished, the big nations to the little nations, the strong nations to the weak, even today, to know that the pagan concept of power is still at work. The serious part of the matter is that if we do not get rid of that pagan concept of power it will surely get rid of us. For neither individuals nor nations who practice it can in the long run prosper. At any rate, it is clearly evident that power is not an unmixed blessing. The very power that has enhanced man's prestige has posed his biggest problem. Just at this moment, when he has never been so strong, he has never been so vulnerable. He has awakened to the fact that he has unwittingly created a sort of Frankenstein which will turn again and rend him. Paul said, "When I am weak, then am I strong"; and it is

[8] Quoted by Will Durant, *The Story of Philosophy,* pp. 441, 466, 468, 470.

always a paradox of faith that an admission of human insufficiency makes one more sufficient. In secularism, on the contrary, man's strength is his weakness, since "pride goeth before destruction, and an haughty spirit before a fall."

Jesus saw this clearly; hence he would not accept that pagan concept of power but gave mankind a new one in which alone is our salvation to be found, namely, power used for service. Said he: "The princes of the Gentiles exercise dominion over them, and they that are great exercise authority upon them. But it shall not be so among you: but whosoever will be great among you, let him be your minister; and whosoever will be chief among you, let him be your servant: even as the Son of man came not to be ministered unto, but to minister, and to give his life a ransom for many." [9] "We then that are strong," says Paul, "ought to bear the infirmities of the weak, and not to please ourselves." Our fathers in their unmechanized age spoke of horsepower. We still use the horse as the symbol of power. In the book of Revelation the name of the man who sat on the horse is called "The Word of God." To put the word of God in the seat of power—that is our salvation. If not, destruction will be our end.

"A Saviour, Christ the Lord"—how strange to put together the words "Saviour" and "Lord"! They seem the antithesis of each other. A savior is like a servant, a lord like a master. A savior comes to serve us, a lord demands that we serve him. A savior comes down to us, a lord is above us. It seems well-nigh paradoxical to combine these two functions in one person. But that is just the mystery of the

[9] Matt. 20:25-28.

200

Christian message, the heart of it: <u>the lordship of saviour-hood</u>; a new concept of greatness, of kingliness, of power—one that reveals itself not in domination or overlordship but in humility and service. God born in a stable, a Saviour who is a Lord. From what death and destruction might we yet be saved would we but accept Christ's concept of power!

I regard Jesus then as the Saviour of the world because he has oriented our thinking upon every great ethical issue —wealth, race, power, and others that could be mentioned —and has given us new ethical goals. The conflicts and tragedies in which we are constantly involved are not always the result of our innate wickedness. Wars, for example, come not so much because the world is full of wicked, beastly people as because it is dominated by inadequate, self-defeating goals. We have posited objectives that are not worthy of our loyalties. The social goals to which we are now committed simply cannot be made to work in God's world. They deny the essentially spiritual nature of man. They flout the fatherhood of God and make shipwreck of the law of love and compassion. It is amusing even to the point of being ridiculous for people to say that our Christian ideals will not work. When we speak that way we naïvely assume that our pagan ideals do work. In a world that is half destroyed because of our secularized, materialistic principles, and that bids fair to be wholly destroyed unless we radically change these principles, we still talk of how impractical Christianity is! One might well ask what could be more impractical than the materialistic policies and goals to which our civilization gives its allegiance. Is it not clearly evident now that our hope of salvation lies in changing them? Are not two world wars in one generation, and the impending danger of a third, enough to convince us of this? I speak therefore confidently of Christ as the Saviour of the world because he posits ideals that are not self-defeating but life-giving.

Finally, we may think of Jesus as our Saviour not only in a personal and social sense but in a cosmic sense. This is the meaning of the statement at the very beginning that were there not something theologically unique about the Christ he would possess no unique ethical significance for mankind. There is something cosmic about this life. It is only because Jesus is our Saviour in the cosmic sense that he is our Saviour in any sense. The type of life he lived and revealed, both for the individual and for society, is not one that he arbitrarily invented. The proof of this lies in the fact that when we reject his way we do not live, we die. Christ has revealed the life that God intends us to live. It is cosmic; the universe supports it. In this Man, I am convinced, a ray of eternity broke through the mists of time. God's eternal word became flesh, to tabernacle with men.

See how timeless his life is! Writes the able theologian Karl Heim: "In the long succession of historical personalities who rise up majestically like pillars of smoke, and then disappear in a higher stratum of air, leaving behind only the lustre of memory, there is one sole exception. There is One Who can say, 'I am with you alway.' " Other men say things that are true for one age but become obsolete in another, are appropriate for one race or culture but not for another. Not so this Man. Never did his words seem more true or inescapable than they do today.

Not only is there a timeless element here, but a universal element. Think of the followers of Jesus, among them Paul, a Hebrew; Francis of Assisi, a Florentine; Lincoln, an American; Tolstoi, a Russian; Kagawa, a Japanese; Schweitzer, an Alsatian—in short, men of every race under heaven.

> In Christ there is no East nor West,
>   In him no South or North;
> But one great fellowship of love
>   Throughout the whole wide earth.

Moreover, among his followers are the very rich and the very poor, the learned and the ignorant, the socially prominent and the humble. He speaks the common language of the human soul, which drowns out all our different dialects.

> In him shall true hearts everywhere
>   Their high communion find;
> His service is the golden cord
>   Close binding all mankind.

The cosmic significance of Jesus' life is seen too in the fact that there is power in this personality. I cannot explain it, nor can you, but though when we compare our lives with the life of Christ we exclaim with Peter, "Depart from me; for I am a sinful man, O Lord," still there is something in Christ which bridges the gap between himself and us, and inspires, encourages, and empowers us to become more like him. There is power in this life to enable man to do what man of himself has never been able to do. Any man who faces the evils that this book has sought to portray, and then thinks that he can blow on his hands, roll up his sleeves, and proceed to eliminate them from society and, most of all, from his own heart is, as the Apostle James might say, thinking of himself more highly than he ought to think. It is my profound faith that in Christ, God has made available the power that is necessary for man's salvation from sin and death. "To will is present with me; but how to perform that which is good I find not." So wrote Paul. But the strength which he could not muster he found available through Christ. "I can do all things through Christ which strengtheneth me." "As many as received him, to them gave he power to become the sons of God." As Professor Walter Marshall Horton has written in *Realistic Theology*: "He did something more centrally important for human deliverance than any philosopher, scientist, or social reformer can possibly do: he broke the power of sin, suffering, and death to corrupt and cow men's souls; and he let loose into the world a great torrent of divine life, love, and power, which is bound in the end to sweep all obstacles away before its onrush."

It is that "torrent of divine life," always available, that is the basis of our hope. Jesus is not simply a figure of history; he is our contemporary. The Jesus of history has become the Christ of faith and experience. He is a Christ whom you and I can know. And the success of our lives will be measured in terms of coming to know him, and God through him, and the world's need through him, and man through him, and ourselves through him—until we attain to the full-grown man, "unto the measure of the stature of the fulness of Christ." As we strive toward that stature we too, by God's grace, may become sharers in his redemptive purpose.